TRADITION^

JOURNEYS ON THE EDGES

TRADITIONS OF CHRISTIAN SPIRITUALITY SERIES

JOURNEYS ON THE EDGES

The Celtic Tradition

THOMAS O'LOUGHLIN

SERIES EDITOR:
Philip Sheldrake

DARTON·LONGMAN+TODD

First published in 2000 by
Darton, Longman and Todd Ltd
1 Spencer Court
140–142 Wandsworth High Street
London SW18 4JJ

ISBN 0–232–52314–2

A catalogue record for this book is available from the British Library.

Phototypeset in 10/13¼pt New Century Schoolbook
by Intype London Ltd
Printed and bound in Great Britain by
Redwood Books, Trowbridge, Wiltshire

In memory of
Sr Paul Brazzill PBVM
(1925–1999)

– a teacher to her fingertips

The sundial at Kilmalkedar. They believed that time is legible: at the point of its fullness Christ appeared (Galatians 4:4) and now they marked time in the final age awaiting his return. This stone told the times of the daytime offices and showed that the monastery's liturgy partook of the order of the heavens.

Behold! we are witnesses to the fact that the gospel has been preached out to those places beyond where any man lives . . . Indeed I have travelled everywhere . . . [and] gone amid many dangers to places beyond where anyone lived. I have gone where no one else had gone to baptise people, or ordain clergy, or complete people.
Patrick, *Confessio* 34 and 51

Brothers, I must make this revelation known to you – lest you be conceited: a blindness has fallen on a part of Israel but only until the full number of the gentile nations is complete, then the whole of Israel will be saved.
Paul, Romans 11:25–6

CONTENTS

PREFACE TO THE SERIES

Nowadays, in the western world, there is a widespread hunger for spirituality in all its forms. This is not confined to traditional religious people let alone to regular churchgoers. The desire for resources to sustain the spiritual quest has led many people to seek wisdom in unfamiliar places. Some have turned to cultures other than their own. The fascination with Native American or Aboriginal Australian spiritualities is a case in point. Other people have been attracted by the religions of India and Tibet or the Jewish Kabbalah and Sufi mysticism. One problem is that, in comparison to other religions, Christianity is not always associated in people's minds with 'spirituality'. The exceptions are a few figures from the past who have achieved almost cult status such as Hildegard of Bingen or Meister Eckhart. This is a great pity, for Christianity East and West over two thousand years has given birth to an immense range of spiritual wisdom. Many traditions continue to be active today. Others that were forgotten are being rediscovered and reinterpreted.

It is a long time since an extended series of introductions to Christian spiritual traditions has been available in English. Given the present climate, it is an opportune moment for a new series which will help more people to be aware of the great spiritual riches available within the Christian tradition.

The overall purpose of the series is to make selected spiritual traditions available to a contemporary readership. The books seek to provide accurate and balanced historical and thematic treatments of their subjects. The authors are also conscious of the need to make connections with contemporary experience and values without being artificial or reducing a tradition to one dimension. The authors are well versed in reliable scholarship about the traditions they describe. However, their intention is that the books should be fresh in style and accessible to the general reader.

One problem that such a series inevitably faces is the word 'spirituality'. For example, it is increasingly used beyond religious circles and does not necessarily imply a faith tradition. Again, it could mean substantially different things for a Christian and a Buddhist. Within Christianity itself, the word in its modern sense is relatively recent. The reality that it stands for differs subtly in the different contexts of time and place. Historically, 'spirituality' covers a breadth of human experience and a wide range of values and practices.

No single definition of 'spirituality' has been imposed on the authors in this series. Yet, despite the breadth of the series there is a sense of a common core in the writers themselves and in the traditions they describe. All Christian spiritual traditions have their source in three things. First, while drawing on ordinary experience and even religious insights from elsewhere, Christian spiritualities are rooted in the scriptures and particularly in the gospels. Second, spiritual traditions are not derived from abstract theory but from attempts to live out gospel values in a positive yet critical way within specific historical and cultural contexts. Third, the experiences and insights of individuals and groups are not isolated but are related to the wider Christian tradition of beliefs, practices and community life. From a Christian perspective, spirituality is not just concerned with prayer or even with narrowly religious activities. It concerns the whole of human life, viewed in terms of a conscious relationship with God, in Jesus Christ, through the indwelling of the Holy Spirit and within a community of believers.

The series as a whole includes traditions that probably would not have appeared twenty years ago. The authors themselves have been encouraged to challenge, where appropriate, inaccurate assumptions about their particular tradition. While conscious of their own biases, authors have nonetheless sought to correct the imbalances of the past. Previous understandings of what is mainstream or 'orthodox' sometimes need to be questioned. People or practices that became marginal demand to be re-examined. Studies of spirituality in the past frequently underestimated or ignored the role of women. Sometimes the treatments of spiritual traditions were culturally one-sided because they were written from an uncritical western European or North Atlantic perspective.

However, any series is necessarily selective. It cannot hope to do full justice to the extraordinary variety of Christian spiritual traditions. The principles of selection are inevitably open to question. I hope that an appropriate balance has been maintained between a sense of the likely readership on the one hand and the dangers of narrowness on the other. In the end, choices had to be made and the result is inevitably weighted in favour of traditions that have achieved 'classic' status or which seem to capture the contemporary imagination. Within these limits, I trust that the series will offer a reasonably balanced account of what the Christian spiritual tradition has to offer.

As editor of the series I would like to thank all the authors who agreed to contribute and for the stimulating conversations and correspondence that sometimes resulted. I am especially grateful for the high quality of their work which made my task so much easier. Editing such a series is a complex undertaking. I have worked closely throughout with the editorial team of Darton, Longman & Todd and Robert Ellsberg of Orbis Books. I am immensely grateful to them for their friendly support and judicious advice. Without them this series would never have come together.

PHILIP SHELDRAKE
Sarum College, Salisbury

INTRODUCTION

In the last decade interest in the attitudes and beliefs of the Christians of the Celtic lands in the first millennium has swollen from being a specialist pursuit among medievalists and historians of theology into what is virtually a popular movement. In the process more than a few books have appeared claiming to uncover the soul of this Celtic Christianity in all its beauty, while still more books have countered this with the view that the whole notion of such a distinctive Christianity is a mirage. Most of the disputants operate by offering their own definitions of 'Christianity' past and present, and then setting these against their definition of 'Celt' or 'Celtic'. In this way they can reach the conclusion they want. The present book does not intend to enter this contest but starts with two assumptions.

First, wherever and whenever Christians are or have been found there have been differences in the ways they have believed and acted upon those beliefs. We can see plenty of examples of this from recent decades, but similar, if slower, shifts in belief and practice have occurred throughout Christianity's history. Thus we speak of 'Patristic theology', 'the medieval Church', and 'Reformation' or 'Counter-Reformation' attitudes. This book is concerned with the period between the great Latin fathers (St Augustine died in 430) and the High Middle Ages (after the twelfth century). This period, the early Middle Ages, has long been recognised as having a distinctive character in terms of its theology and the relationship of religion to society.

My second assumption is that any group of Christians of

common culture and similar attitudes to the larger world beyond themselves will develop a distinctive local flavour to their Christianity despite any attempts they make to avoid such signs of distinctiveness. Again we see this in more recent times: even at the height of the cult of uniformity in early twentieth-century Catholicism, it was recognised that German, Italian and English Catholicism, for instance, could easily be distinguished from each other. So it is not surprising if the people of the north-west fringes of Europe gave their own local flavour to the way they lived out their Christian faith. After all, they had not entered the Roman Empire as migrants, and their language was not Latin but one or other of those we call Celtic.

The question is, can we isolate that flavour from the scraps of evidence that have survived? I am not sure we can do this precisely, but we can identify some of the more widespread characteristics of the Christianity of the period as represented in material from the Celtic lands. My hope is that by doing this we can gather a collection of insights, a window on to that particular part of a past Christian world.

This book is not intended as a history of Christianity in the British Isles in the first millennium; there are several excellent surveys already in existence. Nor is it a systematic account of how the Celts perceived the Christian mystery; such a book is probably an impossibility given the state of our sources. Rather, it is a series of explorations of how 'they', in that time, related to aspects of Christianity in a way that is strange to 'us', now. I shall argue that it is in this process of comparison – and what it can reveal about our spirituality today – that we find the value of looking back to Christianity among the early medieval Celts. The first impression on reaching a foreign country – and that is the way I shall view the past – is to note what is familiar, what 'they' do that 'we' do, what 'they' accept that 'we' accept, and how we are not total strangers. This is a process at which Christians are, on the whole, very good; and it has often suited theological rhetoric to emphasise these continuities. More careful study of a foreign culture reveals just how different it is. Moreover, as many know who travel between two countries with a language and much history in common (for example Britain and the USA), despite all the common elements, the whole – the ensemble – is different. This I think we shall see is the case when the contemporary Christian looks back on the ways of believing and living the Christian life that one finds in the early Middle Ages. They may have recited the same credal formulae that are still in use, but the way they perceived the statements in that creed is, literally, a world away from the way we see them.

The epilogue of this book, pp. 163–4, contains a statement of Christian belief written in Ireland around AD 670. To some it seems a characteristically 'Celtic' piece with its nature imagery; to others it is a typically 'Christian' piece with its technical trinitarian formulae. However, instead of trying to put it in a labelled box, why not just read it, and if you have time jot down a sentence or two on your reactions to it. Then read the book and finish up with it. Read it again and see what now strikes you about the way it presents an image of the Christian God, and see if your perceptions have changed.

When I began to plan and write this book, I noticed that again and again I found myself looking at questions I first heard over the past decade from groups who were exploring the early Christianity of the British Isles and who had asked me for a lecture on this or that topic. To all those people – who often put me on the spot – I wish to say thank you. However, I must reserve a special note of thanks for one group: those whom I have taught over the past five years on the MA in Celtic Christianity here in Lampeter. Meeting with these students again and again, as they became ever more knowledgeable about early medieval texts, and so ever more focused in their questions, I had to confront many of the questions raised in this book which otherwise might have passed me by. To them all, both those on the course at present and those who have graduated, I wish to express my warmest thanks.

1. IS THERE A CELTIC SPIRITUALITY?

<hr>

In those days . . . when Quirinius was governor of Syria . . .
Joseph . . . went up from Galilee, from . . . Nazareth, to
Judea, to the city of David . . . Bethlehem, because he was
of the house and lineage of David . . . with Mary, his
betrothed, who was with child, and while they were there,
the time came for her to be delivered. And she gave birth
to her first-born son and wrapped him in swaddling cloths,
and laid him in a manger. (Luke 2:1–7)

HISTORY AND SPIRITUALITY

These lines from Luke's infancy narrative may seem a strange
place to start a book on the spirituality of the Celtic lands in
the first Christian millennium. Yet, it is only when we understand their inherent sense of history, by which I mean their
sense of events and happenings as being located with the warp
and woof of time and place, that we can appreciate why one
should even attempt to write this book.

The Christian belief that the perfect revelation of God
occurred in Jesus carries with it the implication that the discovery of God occurs within the basic categories of our human
living – that is, space and time. This has been a theme of
theological reflection since, at least, the time of Athanasius (c.
296–373), and a belief that led Christian thinkers to develop
a distinctive Christian theory of space and time. But leaving
aside this speculative strand, there is a far more immediate
dimension to an acceptance that God acts in history.

Whether or not Luke is factually correct when he says that

CHRISTIAN EUROPE AD 600

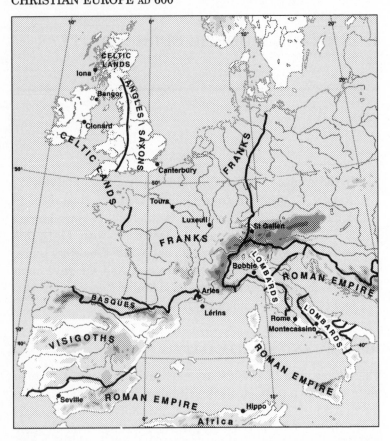

This map shows the major ethnic divisions of Europe that comprise the world in which the spirituality of the Celtic churches emerged.

Jesus was born while Quirinius was governor, or whether the birth actually took place in Bethlehem, is unimportant. What is crucial is Luke's recognition that the Christ had to have a fixed moment of birth, a fixed place, and that Luke's understanding of Jewish expectations assumed a birth in one named town: Bethlehem. To live as an historical being, that is, to be human as we are, is to exist within the limits of the particular and the specific. It is to belong to a family, a place, a culture, and to interact with that culture, benefiting from its good points and being limited by its blind spots.

The Word could not become 'a human' for no such universal being exists. The Word became an actual man, with a moment of birth into a particular family with its own values and peculiarities, and into a community/society that had its specific ways of relating to its inherited Jewish (and indeed Galilean) culture and religion. This man grew to adulthood, like all his contemporaries, within and in interaction with the distinctive political, economic and ethnic conditions of his time and place. This is what it means to exist as a human being: we all have to find our identity within – or in opposition to – the society that rears us both for good and ill. At times we may find this rootedness oppressive and long to create ourselves anew; at other times we take refuge in what is comfortable and familiar – but however we react, we act out of our background. The language we speak, our social environment, our country, our beliefs – any of these may change over a lifetime, yet each new situation is related to what went before it. I am free to choose my tomorrow, yet this freedom is limited by who I am, where I am, and where I have been.

This is what it is to be an historical creature shaping and being shaped by other people and events. I become aware of myself, and my individuality, in the process of trying to understand the context in which I have come into being and live my life. I may have a deep and warm sense of belonging, or (on the other hand) a feeling of being imprisoned, but to come to know the special characteristics of my own time is to appreciate simultaneously my individuality and my relatedness. Of course, such a self-knowledge is never complete, for I can never step outside my own reality and view it as an object in a world 'out there'; yet the attempt is all the more worthwhile, for in the process of searching I come to appreciate what is peculiar to the culture that has shaped me – and I can claim and use the freedom either to adopt my background and 'own it' as what enhances me, or I can 'disown' it as an inherited disability. For most of us our collective past is like our own personal past: in some ways a source of pride and satisfaction, in others a cause of shame and embarrassment.

Like plants in soil, we are affected in every aspect of our lives by our 'growing medium'. And paradoxically, those matters which we tend to think of as most intimate and private – our religious beliefs and outlook on life – are among those most affected, without our being aware of the fact. I may watch the news, conscious of being a westerner, a democrat, a person lucky enough to have been born in the affluent North. But when I express my religious interest (or lack of it), when I try to speak of human love, or use the word 'God', I need to make a conscious and deliberate effort if I am to be aware of my particular reality.

In this book I will assume that the reader is willing to make the effort needed to grasp how a particular culture shaped Christian believing in specific ways. Our own society in the early twenty-first century is affluent, urban, with easy access to global communications; religious interest in the traditional forms of faith is fairly peripheral to everyday life (though there are among us, as in past ages, some people with a very different perception of what it is to live as a follower of Jesus Christ). The people who are the subject of this book were Christians living in Britain, Ireland, and the smaller islands around them, from (roughly) the early fifth century to AD 1000. Those who admire this period call it a 'Golden Age', the 'Age of Saints', the 'Age of the Celtic Church'; others refer to these centuries as the 'Dark Ages' or the period of 'medieval barbarism'. I am using the term 'early medieval' in an attempt to be neutral.

THE GENIUS OF THE PARTICULAR

That a culture in the past can be both 'other' and 'Christian' calls for some comment. In the past many Christians – especially churchmen and theologians – held that Christianity was a religion that cut across nationalities and cultures: one was Christian or non-Christian, and anything that was culture-specific amounted to an impurity, an instance of 'syncretism'.

This, a derogatory word for the 'mixing' of 'other' religious elements with 'pure Christianity', was thought of in terms of a criminal adding base metal to pure gold or silver currency. There was an assumption that Christianity was a religion that appeared whole and entire in the first century AD and that its views on every situation were contained in the New Testament. Thus when it was noticed that, some centuries later, prayers to saints were being said (for instance, in the great litany procession invoking the protection of saints by name on 25 April, which was the date of a pagan Roman ceremony), this had to be seen as Christianity being mingled with pagan ideas from Greece, Rome, Gaul or Ireland. This mingling could be viewed indulgently: the Christian Church could be excused for adopting these trappings – baptising elements which it could not wholly eradicate – so that the gospel message could reach the 'simple' people who were so attached to these 'rude customs'. This is the 'country bumpkin' model of conversion. Another view was that in the lust for power, influence and converts the Church failed to recognise that Christ's religion conflicts with every other notion – which among the extreme holders of this position would be seen as products of the devil – and that the Church compromised faith with superstition. This is the 'all-or-nothing' model of conversion.

In contrast with both views I shall work on the assumption that one cannot isolate Christianity from the cultures in which its adherents live. Thus the early Christians in Egypt and those who heard Paul preach in Asia Minor differed in the style of their response to the gospel message. Equally the reaction to the gospel from a young person in Britain today will be very different from that of someone in Asia or Africa, or from her or his grandparents. It cannot be otherwise, for in the words of the old adage about human knowing, 'Whatever is received is received according to the mode of reception of the receiver.'

The notion that there is a 'pure Christianity' was not destroyed along with nineteenth-century fundamentalism. While, on the whole, theologians and religious writers expect a wide variety of local responses to the gospel and see 'inculturation' (the process by which Christianity takes on a particular colouring depending on the needs of a particular society) as a positive process, many who write about the past have a view of Christianity that is little more than what they learned at Sunday school or have picked up haphazarly without formal study. The same assumption that found 'impurities' in the Christianity of the early Middle Ages, now finds 'pagan survivals' in the writings and practices of the period. While earlier religious writers wondered if those early medieval Christians were 'really disciples' or whether they 'really had faith', many contemporary researchers suggest that maybe the Christian thing was just a veneer. Indeed, since early medieval people still enjoyed 'pagan' stories and customs 'barely disguised by using Christian terms' (whatever that means, it is the obverse of the older notion of 'a baptised custom'), perhaps they considered Christianity as largely irrelevant to their lives? In response to all such notions – and I seem to hear variants of the approach in every television programme or newspaper that mentions the Celts – one can only point out that there has never been a 'pure Christian', but only individuals who have tried to make sense of the mystery of life, love, sorrow and death. Men and women who have given formal allegiance to Christian faith still have to call on every source of information and understanding to try to express themselves – and still they do not encompass reality with their words or ceremonies.

METHOD

Envisage a questionnaire which asked the following:

(a) What is the significance to you of believing that 'the Word became flesh and dwelt among us' (John 1:14)?

(b) How does the history/account of the creation (Genesis 1 and 2), the flood (Genesis 6 – 8), and the re-population of the earth after it (Genesis 9 and 10) affect your view of yourself and your ancestors?

(c) How does your belief that the Lord will come again 'to

judge the living and the dead' (2 Timothy 4:1) affect the
way you plan for the future?

How would we reply? The answers would not just reveal our
attitude to Christian tradition or whether or not we had
studied theology, but would give an insight into our hopes and
fears, and those of the society in which we live. The same
questions could have been posed to everyone who has used the
name 'Christian' as part of their identity since the first century.
Yet while each would have understood the questions, and
indeed would have recognised the very language of the questions as part of their Christian inheritance, just imagine the
variety of answers.

Those in earliest times thought that the Second Coming was
imminent and Paul recommended that they order their lives
accordingly. Later, during the persecutions, the notion that the
Lord would finally bring justice came to the fore to sustain
people. In other situations the Word becoming flesh was seen
as the core of a doctrine of the sacraments so that the Lord
could be 'really present'. At other times, for St Francis of Assisi
for example, for the Word to allow himself to be born was an
expression of divine abasement intended to call us away from
material involvements. More recently it has been seen as an
expression of the value that God places on material creation,
for the Word wholly entered into it. For most Christians down
the centuries the stories of Genesis were simply the earliest
known events of human history. They provided a framework
of 'ages' through which the universe was progressing towards
Jesus and onwards now to the end. They also told of our most
ancient ancestors, and the names of Noah's sons were placed
on maps as the name of the original fathers of each area of
the globe. In such ways the stories provided a sense of time
and place, allowing various local legends to be harmonised
with a 'universal history'. Today, if we make any personal
sense of those stories, it is as moments in the development of
Israel's religious sense rather than as something that speaks
to us directly of our past. Yet, despite the variety of answers,

we are dealing in every case with people who call themselves Christians, who are seeking to a greater or lesser extent to be disciples, who consciously and conscientiously profess their faith, and in every period and culture there are some who even stake their life upon its truth. Would any of us dare to say that we had the right to determine that some were 'Christians' while others were only 'part-Christian' or just 'ignorant bumpkins'?

In the imaginary questionnaire our focus was on the significance of Christianity to an individual within a society. Put another way, it asks how does believing in Jesus Christ affect the way we live our life, explain our surroundings, relate to other people, and mould our hopes and desires. This larger significance of believing men and women as members of a society I shall refer to as 'spirituality'. If theology seeks to make sense of the internal structure of the Christian message, and to make the search for truth as an intellectual quest based on Christian faith, then a study of spirituality is an examination of how cultures have reacted to that Christian proclamation. It seeks to understand the ways that Christians here and there in the past have made their belief life-giving or life-restricting, and how Christians in the present can relate their lives to that Christian message in accordance with their personality, circumstances and culture. This book is an attempt to ascertain how Christians in the Celtic lands might answer that questionnaire if we could travel back and present it to them.

ATTRACTIONS

But why bother? Well, first of all there is basic intellectual curiosity. I am not only intrigued by the past as an historian, but I want to know how people of past ages thought, how they represented the world to themselves, how they imagined the holy, and how they saw the boundaries between their ordinary lives and the supernatural. This is as legitimate a question as how they farmed or fought or governed themselves – although getting answers to my questions is a far more elusive business. A second reason for looking at spiritualities from the past is that for Christians the past is like a vast store-house of experience from which we can extract ways of believing and behaving that can either inspire or warn us for the present. Indeed, since there is no such thing as an ideal Christian or ideal church (except as a mental invention), if we want to get a perspective on our situation today we must use historical Christians (each a mixture of good and bad) and churches (all of which heard parts of the gospel while forgetting other parts) as the basis for comparative assessments. Against some of these we can see elements of discipleship of which we are acutely aware while they passed them by, or forgot them altogether; but against other aspects of the past we find that we are the ones who are lacking. The past can have the beneficial effect of relativising our present concerns, and forcefully dispelling any notion that we represent some peak of human excellence towards which all previous times are just a prologue.

A third reason for examining past spiritualities lies in our relationship to them: we have inherited from earlier times much of our Christian world-view; and often attitudes that made sense in one situation are outmoded and we failed to recognise this. In seeing where we have come from, we have a new understanding of our historical identity and are given the key to release ourselves from slavery to it. Lastly, we can gain wisdom for our own discipleship. This is sometimes dismissed as adolescent atavism on the basis that the past is past and foreign. But we should note that it was that desire to gain wisdom from earlier Christians that inspired hagiography down the centuries. If every age has to make sense of the mystery of the revelation of God, then we are not only bound to long-dead Christians through the communion of saints in Christ, but by the fact that the mystery is equidistant to every age and culture. Visiting the Church of the past is not so much entering a museum as returning to the same wells that were signposted long ago.

So why the spirituality of the Celtic lands? No answer to this question can be satisfactory, for the reasons attracting us to study one topic rather than another always lie deep inside us. However, we can note a few general factors. Many who read this book will identify in one way or another with the Christians of these islands in the first millennium – they are our ancestors. To look at them is to look at our past, our culture, it is to locate us within a specific people and place. For others, there is the attraction of a 'lost wisdom', a sense that somehow the unique insights of early Ireland, Scotland and Wales represent an ancient alternative, for it appears that these insights did not become part of the standard western forms of Christianity as found in the last couple of centuries. Sales of books claiming to recover 'an ancient Celtic wisdom' show how widespread is this attraction. Historians may debunk such claims by pointing out that what really distinguishes this 'wisdom' from much modern Christianity amounts to little more than its reflecting pre-Reformation concerns – for the most distinctive elements of insular Christian practice (for example, the penitentials) became standard parts of western Christianity – but this does not vitiate the desire to uncover a sharper Christian vision from beneath what is seen as the accretion and debris of the present. The attempt to recover a new purity through going back to the past can be seen in the composition of Deuteronomy at the time of Josiah's reforms, in Luke's myth of a pristine early community, in many 'reform' movements in monasticism, and in the quest for 'the purity of Celtic spirituality'. Somehow the idea that we can look back to the kind of religion we need for today and tomorrow makes achieving our desires seem less problematic.

Finally, I should note that an important element of the attractiveness of the spirituality of the Celtic lands lies in seeing parts of its legacy around us: strange ruins in the countryside, beautiful manuscripts and metalwork, hearing the odd lovely prayer used in liturgy. This creates a special curiosity, for it overlaps with our curiosity about place – what happened long ago where we live today. This is the key attraction in local history: we know better where we are today if we know our place's past. So too with religion, we can have a deeper understanding of our Christianity if we are aware of the Christians who followed the Lord here in the very places where we walk.

HISTORY AS A REFLECTION

Now we come up against the problem which underlies this whole book: if we want to know about the spirituality of the Celts, how can we discover it? In the case of a contemporary spirituality I could either pose a set of questions and learn of a person's particular 'take' on Christianity through discussion with them or read the thoughts of those who write about it in a formal way. Both options are excluded for the past: the first is obviously unavailable, but equally the second. Christians in the first millennium did not use the category of 'spirituality' in their writings. The closest they came to such a distinction was in their formal exegesis of Scripture where 'historical' exegesis dealt with the text's original meaning, 'spiritual' exegesis dealt with what it revealed about Jesus Christ (and to an extent the destiny of our souls), while 'moral' exegesis dealt with the actual moral rules to be derived from Scripture. However, the very formality of exegesis makes it less than useful in discovering how those earlier Christians approached the meaning of Christianity for their lives.

So this book will have to try to extract that picture from evidence that was written to carry a different message to a very different audience. It will try to 'overhear' discussions of the Christian life and see if, from a slant here or an odd comment there, we can construct a mosaic that may explain the celts and their discipleship. In any work of medieval history there are two processes at work. First, we try to isolate little bits of evidence that tell us of the detail of people's lives and beliefs – we can think of this as Sherlock Holmes going around with his magnifier and tweezers. Second, we construct an overall picture of individuals and of a society out of the bits that have survived. This is like a jig-saw puzzle where we have lost a great many pieces: we have to get the surviving pieces into roughly the correct place and then sketch in the gaps. This is all the more difficult when the particular picture is that of a spirituality: it does not leave remains that survive in the same way as does, say, the evidence of a people's political life.

We cannot construct a detailed picture of the spirituality of the Celts, for we simply do not have enough evidence. Rather, our pictures hold up a reflection of *our* own concerns: we can learn only incidentally about how *they* saw these issues. Here I must sound the warning bell. Notions such as 'the Celtic Church' and 'Celtic spirituality' are common currency at present: there are books, articles, seminars and courses on the subject. In many of these there are confident assertions that 'the Celts believed' or 'the Celts had a different way of looking, or doing, or acting, or . . .'. Such general statements are simply nonsense.

First, what we know about the paganism of the Celtic lands – which figures prominently in many books on 'Celtic spirituality' – is meagre indeed. Classical pre-Christian sources, on the one hand, naturally tend to project what the Greeks thought a 'primitive religion' should be. Posidonius the Stoic is the most quoted source, and, behold, the Celtic religion comes close to what Stoics held was basic to religion. The other sources are Christian, for example Muirchú's *Life of Patrick* from *c.* 680, but in these texts the pagan forebears show a remarkable resemblance to the Baal followers in 1 Kings and the Persians in the book of Daniel!

Second, what has survived are the fragments of a complex world. Time is a blind sieve. It loses (or saves) both good and bad – and we cannot say even whether we have good and bad in equal measure. All the texts that might reveal the spirituality of the Celts were hand-copied for more than half their history, and any work that is not in use tends to be forgotten; if it survives it is a matter of chance. Even societies that have had a relatively stable urban life for centuries, for instance

northern Italy, lose materials over time; how much more when
there were the disruptions of the Vikings, the Normans, and
then the Reformation. We have texts, artefacts and sites but
think how much more there was in the period we are concerned
with. It is worth remembering that every little church had a
missal and a chalice and a paten – minimum equipment. Yet
today we have only one intact missal from early medieval
Ireland (the Stowe Missal), we have two chalices (both
beautiful works, but both found by accident), and one paten
(found with one of the chalices at Derrynaflan, Co. Tipperary
in 1980).

Third, these people did not write with our concerns in mind,
and what they did, was written in a society very different from
our own. 'The past is a foreign country', and we must not
assume that what we take for granted is true for them. We
should feel a constant jarring between their values and ours,
their likes and ours, their blind-spots and our own. When
any early medieval text feels warm and cosy to our religious
sensibilities, then we should watch out. Many popular books
suggest that the Celts had exactly what we need and want –
all it needs is to have the dust taken off it! Such notions are
simply flights of fancy. It is always refreshing to look at a
spirituality that is foreign to our own, it makes us sit up and
examine our assumptions. But we can never simply adopt
other spiritualities, for *my* next step must start from where I
am now. And because the past is foreign, and its spirituality
pieced together, there are areas of it we can never understand
or appreciate. Bede, for example, found saints' lives to be enjoyment and relaxation after serious theology; most people today
find them some of the dullest writings that have survived! If
we were to draw up a list of such dissonances, it would be a
long one.

HISTORY AS SEARCH

If we have only bits and pieces, from here and there, separated
from us in time and strange to us in world-view, should we

even try to understand them? Well, while we cannot say that 'it was always like this or that' or that 'Celts believed this or that' – because our fragments are scattered over time and come from different religious settings – we can get a flavour of the period. The analogy is looking back at photographs or videos of a holiday: they do not record everything, but they convey an impression of the whole trip. I like the word 'snap-shots'. We do not see the entire holiday but get a snapshot of the hotel, the places visited, some of the people we met, and ourselves doing this or that. The texts that survive from the early medieval period are like snapshots of *their* religious adventure. My hope is that each chapter of this book is a snapshot, and that taken together they make up an album that conveys parts of the larger picture.

History is not like rummaging in an attic to puzzle over items we have discarded. History as a search for answers is like making enquiries in a foreign country whose language one does not understand. If, because the past is alien, we come to believe that we should not even try to reconstruct it, however imperfectly, then which will be the next dialogue we regard as not worth the effort? Soon we would be reduced to isolated silence. The 'other' – be it someone beside us or someone who wrote in Latin over a thousand years ago – will always be greater than our understanding, but it is the effort to com-municate and understand the depths of the other that makes us spiritual beings.

The study of an alien past is especially valuable in the case of Christian spirituality. People long ago and people today are seeking to be disciples, relating to the same basic texts in Scripture, and holding the same events as central to faith, so through the common elements we can see ourselves more clearly: noting what the earlier group had, that we have lost; and what we have, about which they never dreamed. For them the power of God in the universe was unproblematic – the monks who lived on Iona saw the Lord's power on the mighty waters (Psalm 29:3) every day of their lives. But equally the notion that the Lord could forgive and enable a new beginning to take place in the life of a sinner – something we preach day in and day out – was something they were only searching for, fearful that they would break faith with some of the teachings of the fathers. To us, obedience is problematic, but to them it was an obvious essential. We think we are daring when we say that the Spirit moves in every human heart leading it towards Christ, whereas they seem to have taken it as a theological first premise – as we shall see when we look at Muirchú. When we look back at how earlier Christians believed and lived their faith in Christ, it is the parts of their spirituality that strike us as strange that are most instructive.

A PATH OR WALKERS

Because we are dealing with fragments and trying to overhear the conversations of faith of a past era, there can be no question of producing a 'Celtic Path' of spirituality. A path assumes that you can cover the ground, and map its ups and downs, and give a fullsome description. Rather, we are going to look at individual events and texts on different topics: we are going, as it were, to chat to walkers here and there along the path which we cannot see in its entirety. This path reaches over several centuries and on it we meet up with monks and clerics and lay women and men. We will look at popular works such as the *Journey of Brendan* (the *Nauigatio sancti Brendani*) and the *Life of Patrick* (the *Vita Patricii*) by Muirchú. We will look at bits of law and pastoral manuals, some prayers and homilies, and some other things besides. Each glimpse is a snapshot and they are put together here in a collage. You can dip into the work chapter by chapter in whatever order strikes you as most interesting. This is not a documentary on 'What is Celtic spirituality?'; it is a collection of stills and trailers on how some Christians have perceived their discipleship. It is up to you to arrange the collage and sketch the larger picture – and then to decide if it can be labelled 'Celtic spirituality'.

2. A WALK IN TWO WORLDS

I asked the earth and it answered: 'I am not he' . . . I asked
the sea and its creatures and they answered: 'We are
not your God, seek higher!' I asked the whole air, and
everything in it, and it answered: 'Anaximenes was wrong
– I am not your God.' I asked the heavens, the sun, moon
and stars, and they answered: 'Neither are we God whom
you seek.' . . . I asked the whole frame of the universe
about my God and it answered me: 'I am not he, but he
made me.' (Augustine, *Confessions* 10.6)

ALL THE WORLD'S A SIGN

One of the attractive features of early medieval writings for
us today is their sense of the closeness of God as manifested
in the beauty and rhythms of nature. This is something that
is foreign to much of the Christianity that we have received.
We may sing 'all creatures great and small' but this is a
children's hymn, and it is little more than stating in a homely
way our belief in creation's origin in God. So foreign indeed is
this strand of rejoicing in the glory of the creation that some
have seen it as a pagan legacy, a nature worship, or as the
rejection of any distinction between matter and spirit. Another
of the attractions of Celtic writings is a sense of forlorn remoteness we experience when we think about these people. We see
them as people on the edge: monks living on windswept islands
such as Iona off Scotland, Holy Island off Northumbria, Caldey
and Bardsey off Wales, or Skellig Michael and Inisbofin off
Ireland. We have an instant picture of a monastic spirit that

flees the world of people in favour of the desert where, in their search of God, they will confront themselves and evil. These themes of creation and remoteness are intimately connected, and this chapter is an attempt to explore them.

One of the central themes of Christianity in the first millennium, both East and West, is that the world around us, and our very selves, are marked through and through with the imprint of our maker. This universe has all over it, from the heavens above down to the smallest detail on earth, the tell-tale signs of something infinitely greater, beyond it, before it, and giving it purpose. In each thing there are the 'footprints' of the Creator, and from these things humans can recognise that there is a God, and that there is an order in creation. These Christians took their lead from Paul writing to the Romans: 'For what can be known about God is plain to them, because God has shown it to them. Ever since the creation of the world his invisible nature, namely, his eternal power and deity, has been clearly perceived in the things that have been made' (1:19–20). But the creation is not just there with its maker's marks upon it, it is there in this way precisely so that human beings, the focus of the creation, could look around them and learn, through reflection on the visible creatures surrounding them, of their origin and end. The universe was to be treated like a book. A book tells you about something greater than the words on the page; it is a recollection of something more real than itself. Just think that now you are reading this, but this is only a memory of the beliefs of those early Christians; they and their beliefs existed, and these words only exist as a shadow of those beliefs. So the 'book' of the creation spoke of its author and communicated his most basic characteristics. Here lies the basis of what some modern writers have detected as the 'eco-friendliness' in the early medieval Christianity that we are studying. We could describe this more accurately if we extended the book metaphor: if the creation is a book written by God, to be deciphered by humans in prayerful reflection, then one should turn its pages gently.

SIGNS AND THINGS: AUGUSTINE

By the time that we see Christianity flourishing in the Celtic
lands, from the later fifth century, this notion of the sacramental quality of the universe had been articulated
theoretically by Augustine (354–430), as a simple formula that
could be communicated easily to ordinary Christians by Eucherius of Lyons (who died mid-fifth century), and as part of
the life of monastic Christian perfection by John Cassian (c.
360–435). Augustine is not usually put in the company of the
other two writers, and it would have shocked some in the later
fifth century to see them linked. Yet for those who came after
them in Ireland and Wales there was little difficulty in weaving
their ideas together: they lived with the notion that the universe is a sign, a pointer, a sacrament of the Word through
whom it is made, and who enters that creation out of love for
humanity to redirect us to our End.

Augustine had laid out his sacramental vision of reality
quite soon after his baptism and, on this point at least, he
hardly altered his opinion. His starting point was the distinction between 'signs' and 'realities'. Realities existed for
themselves, but signs, while real things, referred the observant
human being to something greater. So to one who knows its
nature, smoke points to combustion, and the word and sound
of 'd-o-g' represents a small quadruped such as many people
keep as pets. But just as we use signs as part of being human
– words, symbols, metaphors – so God has ordained that the
whole universe will address us in this manner. Everything had
been made in a well-ordered way by the Creator in 'order, and
number, and weight' (Wisdom 11:21). So whenever we look at
a creature (that is, everything other than God) we should not
just find matter, a neutral stuff we can do with what we like,
but rather something that has order within it. Creatures have
an order and purpose within them, the seed grows to be a tree
and lives on in ordered cycles. The heavens move in an orderly
way and bring the seasons, and so bring growth and harvest.
Every living being is a wonder of complexity yet it carries out

its task, for the Lord 'has sweetly and powerfully disposed all things, ordering them from one end of the universe to the other' (Wisdom 8:1). Whenever we see order – this is more than simple regularity, it is complex things 'coming together' in harmony – then if our eyes are open (the gift of faith) we do not just marvel at this wonder, but are drawn beyond the order to the Orderer. Equally, everything we see can be described in number. There is one creation, so many stars, the heavens can be predicted through their numbered regularity, everything material can be measured. We must not just be fascinated with such arithmetic, but know that anything that can be numbered is limited, so beyond the numbered universe is the Being-beyond number, the true Infinity of being, beauty and power. Likewise, material things all have a definite place in the creation. The world around us is not just a jumbled heap, so there is an organising principle even in these things. Augustine referred to this using the scriptural term 'weight'. This means that in even the least interesting bit of matter, there is a link to God, for it would not be where it is without the divine creative will which gave it its 'weight', its place in the whole scheme of things.

For Augustine, when we look around the material world we should be able to see two levels of reality: the beautiful, ordered creatures, and beyond them the mystery that gives them being. Here was the task of Christians: to raise their sights from looking 'downwards' on the creation as something just there, to the beauty/order/number that is inherent in it, and then even higher to the Giver of its beauty. Faith was a task of seeing through corporeal things to arrive at the incorporeal. But here also lay the temptation for humanity. One could become so fascinated with the creation that one became engrossed, and failed to see that it is not an end in itself but the work of Another. Humans can use the creation and even enjoy it, but such enjoyment is transitory. The only enjoyment that is not marred by a limit is in God.

Augustine thought that the history of humanity's beliefs was a tale of this confusion of creature with Creator, of passing things that are to be used as gifts and signs being treated as realities that are to be enjoyed for ever. This had happened to the Israelites when they made the Golden Calf (Exodus 32) and 'exchanged the glory of God for the image of an ox that eats grass' (Psalm 106:20), and Augustine believed the process of distraction was laid out in detail in Wisdom 13. When the wisdom of the Greeks had led them to number the heavens accurately, they became so amazed by the numbering that they thought that the order itself was divine and powerful and so became slaves of astrology. Christians must be aware of a tension in their lives: they must value the creation as God's gift and a precious sacrament pointing them back to the Alpha and forward to the Omega, but they must not stop short at the sacrament, they must look beyond to the God towards whom the cosmos points.

GOD'S CODE: EUCHERIUS

Eucherius, although only slightly younger than Augustine, was a very different sort of man. Augustine, Bishop of Hippo, gives the impression of being on fire, a man of extremes. Eucherius, who died as Bishop of Lyons, conveys a sense of urbanity and moderation in everything. He and his wife decided they would retreat from the world to the island monastery of Lérins, and for many years they and their children lived there. He certainly knew of Augustine, and had read him, but he never mentions Augustine by name – a polite snub for his writings aimed at correcting some of the extreme positions of the older Augustine. Later, Eucherius was called from Lérins – which he considered an idyllic place – to be a bishop, and later again both his sons became bishops of nearby dioceses.

It was probably while the family lived on Lérins that Eucherius wrote his two short works on what we call spirituality: *On contempt of the world* (*De contemptu mundi*) and *In praise of the desert* (*De laude heremi*). Their titles may be off-putting, but their message is similar to the sacramentalism of Augustine. There is beauty everywhere in the creation, for it reflects the beauty of God, if only we can see it. The life of calm reflection, of withdrawal from business and cares is not a flight from the world inspired by revulsion, but rather a movement to give oneself – and in his case his wife and children – the 'space' to appreciate the goodness of God in the creation, and then to appreciate God. The world can fill us with business, distracted like Martha over many things (Luke 10:41), but it can also provide us with the means to recollect ourselves and see, in our wonder, the glory of God. There is a gentleness in Eucherius that makes his notions of 'flight from the world' and his 'deserted place' on Lérins far more appealing than the extremes described in some of the lives of the desert fathers. However, the little book that would make Eucherius famous for five hundred years, and make him one of the most used authorities in the scriptural exegesis in early Christian Ireland, was written after he left Lérins for Lyons.

Aware of the needs of preachers who had to interpret Scripture, Eucherius produced his *Formula for a spiritual understanding* (*Formula spiritalis intellegentiae*) which enabled one who knew the work to see through the surface (historical) level of Scripture to its 'higher' spiritual meaning. He noted all sorts of things mentioned in the Scriptures from natural objects like the sun, moon, trees, fire, stones and animals, human objects like fields, houses, all the parts of the body, various numbers and references to places and actions; and then he found somewhere else in the Scriptures where that same object was used in a clearly metaphorical way. Eucherius then latched on to that symbolic meaning, and declared that that was its deeper meaning throughout God's revelation. So, for example, when we meet the word 'field' (*ager*) in the Scriptures (it occurs 253 times) what does it mean? Christ (what better interpreter could there be?) tells us that it signifies this world of ours (Matthew 13:38). So whenever we meet 'field' (upon the authority of Scripture itself) we can read this word as a code pointing to a higher realm where to those who know the code, it means 'the world'.

What Eucherius had done was to create a two-tier world for

Scripture: there was the text you could read on the page in front of you, and there was the more real, more permanent and higher meaning to which it pointed through its symbols/ codes. The text, the 'letter' to use Paul's image (2 Thessalomians 2:2), was a veil through which Christians had to move until they reached the world beyond the physically visible; this was spiritual knowing. Eucherius was in line with a pattern of interpreting Scripture that had been developing since before the time of Jesus – and which affected many of the New Testament writers themselves – but he brought this sacramentalist view of the text to a new level both theoretically and practically. The Scriptures stood on the edge of this fragile material world and offered a vision of a more lasting world. It was a vision with which Eucherius inspired countless Christians in the Celtic lands just as later, having been ignored by the scholastics, he inspired the Welsh/English poet Henry Vaughan (1622–1695) and, more recently, Thomas Merton (1915–1968).

Since the Scriptures used images from this world, yet told of heaven, the very things in the world could, for those with the eyes of faith, be symbols of a higher world. The whole material world could be a parable, not in words but things, to be decoded in the same way as the parables in the Gospels. This was the next logical development of the theory, combining the cosmic sacramentalism of Augustine with the textual sacramentalism of Eucherius. So that whether one read the Scriptures or walked down the lane to work in the fields or just looked out of one's window, one could take all that entered the mind as both real (in a transient earthly/physical way) and as the shimmering image of the higher heavenly world. This world was now, for the Christian, just hovering on the edge of being. The call to the Christian was to move to its very limit and peer beyond. This could take place in reflection while walking and working, or in decoding the Scriptures, and in the liturgy Christians could actually experience praising God with the inhabitants of that higher world: the angels and powers, the cherubim and seraphim, the choir of the apostles and prophets, and the white-robed army of martyrs (cf. the *Te Deum*). Whether walking, working, reading or praying, one was in two worlds: this physical world which seemed so real but which was fragile and slipping away moment by moment, and the spiritual world which was intangible, clouded the senses, but which was real; and if one 'had not a lasting city here' (Hebrews 13:14), then it was by no means certain that one had yet been granted a place 'in the kingdom' (Matthew 5:19). Christian life was in many senses a journey along an edge.

ASCETIC SACRAMENTALISM: CASSIAN

The third major influence on Christianity in Celtic lands was Cassian. A friend of Eucherius, he tailored his accounts of the fathers of the desert to the monastic situation in southern Gaul in such a way that others, throughout the West, found in him the ideal guide to the monastic life. His influence in Celtic lands can be judged by the fact that modern students of insular monasticism are constantly struck by similarities between Celtic practices and those of Eastern monasticism, and especially the monasticism of Egypt and Syria. Alas, the great cries of 'links' between the Celts and the Egyptians, Greeks or Syrians are misplaced: all such Eastern elements can be traced to the mediation of Cassian. Elements once common in the West (brought there from the East by Cassian), but which did not figure in Benedictine monasticism and which therefore disappeared elsewhere in the ninth century, survived longer in monasteries on the north-western fringe of Europe.

Cassian, like Augustine and Eucherius, used a two-tier arrangement of knowledge, exegesis and the spiritual life. On the lower level there were the things of sense, which were ordered towards praxis, studied by historical exegesis, and belonged to the 'actual life'. Leading on from that lower involvement were the things of the spirit, studied using various levels of spiritual interpretation, which belonged to the 'contemplative life'. As with the other writers' presentations, this is a sacramentalism where this world's value lies in its being the stepping-off point into the realm of the divine. What was unique was that this process was fully part of a life of religious dedication. Both Augustine and Eucherius promoted the religious life, but one could read their writings on knowing and interpreting Scripture and leading the life of faith without seeing any direct link to a life of asceticism or taking on the distinctive lifestyle of the monk. Not so with Cassian: the lower life was part of the everyday world and its engagements; the higher life demanded withdrawal, a purification from its allurements, and a definite decision to centre one's whole life on God. Without such a dedicated plan for discipleship one could at best lead a 'mixed life' where, while one saw beyond the senses, one still treated them as if they had a reality of their own. Within Cassian's view the decision to withdraw from the centre of this world of the senses to its edge, and to remain there, constituted the significant human movement. The closer one was to the centres of this world, the more one was drawn down from the real objects of life and immersed in transient matter.

FATHERS AND SAINTS

Early insular writers took over from Augustine, Eucherius and Cassian this two-tier universe where the material cosmos reflected a higher reality, and Christians possessed in revelation the key to 'read' that higher reality through its sacrament, the lower world around them. Today, we wonder that writers whom we spend time distinguishing, such as Augustine and Cassian, or ignore altogether, such as Eucherius, could be read in this way, but for those early medieval writers what united the three far outweighed their differences. They were the fathers and so they must be part of the harmony of an orchestra. These writers became the great sources, and the theme was then filled out with lives of the desert saints. The first, and paradigmatic, *vita* of Antony of Egypt was written shortly after his death (c. 356) by Athanasius. Athanasius' aim is clear from his preface: if you know Antony's struggles and how he won them, 'you will be able to train with zeal to imitate him'. He assumes that a way of life is better learned by imitation of lifestyle and habit than by a theoretical presentation, 'for Antony's life is an appropriate guide to monks in asceticism'. Translated into Latin *c.* 360 by Evagrius of Antioch, its influence spread through the empire within decades, as Augustine witnesses, and it was a basic text of monastic wisdom in the Celtic lands.

Jerome came next among the writers of monastic hagiography, inspired directly by Athanasius. His life of Paul of Thebes (written *c.* 376) was to determine who was regarded as the first desert hermit. Around 391 Jerome wrote lives of Malchus and Hilarion. While his purpose is moral in all three works, the later ones are more obviously guides to being a hermit, as well as to the routine for a group of ascetics, and are interspersed with the miracles of these Palestinian monks. Their popularity in Ireland can be judged from the fact that Paul is presented as one of the model saints encountered by Brendan on his monastic odyssey – a topic we shall look at more closely in chapter 5.

The third highly influential piece of hagiography was Palladius' *Historia Lausiaca* (*c.* 419–420). Again inspired by Athanasius, Palladius stated his aim as providing learners with models for imitation from those strong in faith and ascetical endurance (*Letter to Lausus*). He supplied 71 such models by name. And, uniquely, Palladius included women among his model saints, even showing them teaching men! His influence can be seen in that his accounts of the stone cells built by Dorotheus as penance probably supplied the idea for the beehive-shaped stone cells built by Irish monks in places like Skellig Michael.

Most people today find these saints' lives repellent: their miracles incredible, and detrimental to faith; their accounts of demons silly, or evidence for psychological disorders (for example *Vita Antonii* 8); while tales involving chastity evidence a profound anti-body fascination. This shift in appreciation vividly illustrates the shift in world-views between the early medieval period and our own. However, it is the manner in which insular Christians combined these hagiographic and monastic sources with a sacramental, virtually Neoplatonic, view of the universe that is one of the most interesting parts of their spirituality.

LIVING IN TENSION

We readily appreciate the negative aspects of much early hagiography, and it has become a commonplace to note the unbalanced nature of most of Jerome's writings on the Christian life. Such criticism was not open to monks in the medieval monastery: these were the accounts of the saints who had been proven, and who now shared 'the inheritance of the saints in light' (Colossians 1:12). The achieved sanctity of those fathers meant that they, and so their lifestyles, must be valued as exemplary. However, the monastic rejection of material things was balanced in the Celtic lands by the need to study that same material world, as it was the book of nature to be interpreted in a manner analogous to the pages of the written law.

From our perspective, we tend to reject spiritualities which stress binary oppositions of matter and spirit, this world and the world to come, the transient and the everlasting, as being tinged with dualism, or at least as not giving sufficient attention to the creation around us. And, if one were to read only the prescriptions for penitence in the penitentials or the accounts of penance in saints' lives, then that judgement would appear justified for the Celtic lands. However, their binary separation of the creation into two worlds is fundamentally different: the relationship between these worlds is not that of a negative and a positive, or a bad/defective world and a good/perfect world – such as one finds in many ancient philosophies and religions – but one of anticipation and fulfilment, of shadow and reality, of pointer and objective, of way and destination. The material existed not as an alternative to the spiritual, but for the sake of the spiritual. It was the place of the journey, and the higher world was the place which beckoned one to start out on the journey, and its destination. In this kind of relationship the lower cannot be ignored nor treated as an illusion or prison: it is the place where one must discover the basic things of God and where one must prove oneself. Likewise, the material world cannot be rejected as evil, for that would be to deny not only that it was the divine handiwork, but also it would involve rejecting the word of God which communicated itself sacramentally through it. The art and skill of the Christian life was to attend to the material not as an end itself (that was the basic sin of distraction that led to false gods and superstition), but as the sacrament of the true homeland.

So 'the narrow way' of the Christian was to journey through life without rejecting the material creation (which would, in effect, be the same as becoming a dualist) and without rejecting the higher reality to which humans were called (becoming a materialist). It was a call to live a life of tense attention; they recognised that it was very easy to be pulled one way or the other, to an extreme which was false. However, in this temptation to extremes their concerns were different from ours. We are more likely to fear that the rejection of the creation would be our downfall as religious people (and so we scorn 'pie in the sky when you die' type of spirituality); they were far more concerned lest instead of seeing through matter to the higher world, they lower their gaze to focus solely on matter. We see this difference, for example, in the concerns of the penitentials with the sinner who has ignored the higher world and become engrossed in the concerns of this life or the body. There is no corresponding set of warnings about the dangers of being so concerned with the spiritual world to come that one ignores the present world and one's duties towards others.

SHADOWS AND THIN PLACES

In several places in the New Testament there is an image that
means very little to us, but which was of enormous significance
in the early Middles Ages, that of the 'shadow' (*skia/umbra*).
We think of a shadow as something left behind, an after-effect,
but in Colossians 2:17 there is the notion that the shadow of
what is to come appears first, and afterwards 'the substance',
which 'belongs to Christ'. In Hebrews 8:5 the rituals from
the time of Moses were regarded as 'a copy and shadow of the
heavenly sanctuary'. Those earlier rituals were copied from
'the pattern which was shown . . . on the mountain', and were
given as an anticipation of the sacrifice of Christ. In Hebrews
there is the implication that all earthly liturgy is the 'shadow'
of the heavenly liturgy. Equally, in Hebrews 10:1 it is declared:
'For since the law has but a shadow of the good things to come
instead of the true form of these realities, it can never, by the
same sacrifices which are continually offered year after year,
make perfect those who draw near.' In these references a
shadow is an anticipation, a fore-type, a taster, and a direction-
setter for the future towards a higher reality, to which we do
not yet have access. We find this notion of 'shadow' in J. H.
Newman's epitaph, *ex umbris et imaginibus in veritatem*,
which has implied motion and must be translated by something like, 'I have moved from shadows and images to the true
realities.' This notion of shadow is intimately connected with
the notion of sacramentality: the sacrament is perceived now,
but only as a sign; the reality for which it stands is both future
and elsewhere.

In this sense the Christians of the early medieval period
could refer to the material creation, the present world, as a
shadow, and see the pattern of shadow-leading-to-reality in
every aspect of their faith. The old covenant was a shadow of
the new, the law a shadow of the gospel, the prophets a shadow
of the Christ, the old liturgy a shadow of the new, the presence of the Word in the creation a shadow of the Word made
flesh, the knowledge of God in nature and pagan religions a

shadow of that preached by the Church. The whole of this world was but a shadow of that to come. As such it was a sacrament within the whole plan of God; and sacraments are precious, and must be handled with respect and in a sacred way. To declare in this sense that this world is but a shadow has probably the opposite effect of denying it in a Platonic or Manichaean fashion – for now the world must be handled with care, and it must be read as a window on mystery.

SACRAMENTAL VALUES

This sacramentalist view of the world affected many other aspects of the world-view of Christians in the Celtic lands. First and foremost it accounts for the 'valuing of the creation' that has attracted so many people to 'Celtic spirituality' in recent years. More perversely, it has led some people to imagine that because 'the Celts' could see that the creation was a revelation of God, this must indicate links with 'paganism'. Such commentators fail to realise that all pre-modern Christianity was fundamentally sacramentalist. Incidentally, we have no evidence that there was anything approaching such a position in the paganism that Christianity replaced. Second, the sacramentalist view of the world enables us to understand the enormous value placed on the sacramental rites of Christianity which we can see in accounts of baptisms in saints' lives or still see in beautiful altar plate such as the Derrynaflan chalice and paten or the Ardagh chalice. By extension, since Scripture was read sacramentally we can understand the value they set on exegesis (decoding the signs) and why the vehicle of that sacrament (the actual book made of parchment) could have such a wealth of art lavished upon it as we see in manuscripts like the Book of Kells or the Golden Book of Echternach.

Today, many, if not most, Christians reject all of the physics and much of the exegesis of Scripture upon which that early medieval sacramentalism was based. Moreover, for many Christians even the very notion of sacraments is problematic.

What one person sees as a step towards another dimension, another Christian sees as a ritualised obstacle between the individual and God. Moreover, a consequence of a sacramental view is that one must value the community where sacred signs are treasured and decoded, and so one must see the community, the Church, as itself sacramental. But this notion that to be a Christian is to belong to a group is also a problem for many people, for there has been an emphasis on religion as an individual activity in much Christian preaching in recent centuries.

However, even allowing for these difficulties, that view of the world from long ago has still much to teach us. It can give a religious perspective to our ecological concerns and our desires to value the material universe as sacred, while avoiding the trends present in many New Age and neopagan cults where the earth itself becomes the object of worship and is believed to be the source of spiritual power. Equally, it can remind us of the basic Christian belief that the Word is at work in the creation from the beginning and that all matter is 'stamped' with the mark of its Originator. As the early Christian hymn used by John, and echoed in the creeds, says: the Word 'was in the beginning with God; all things were made through him, and without him was not anything made that was made' (John 1:2–3). Therefore our exploitation of the material creation as some neutral stuff at our disposal is incompatible with that belief in the creation. At the same time, the memory of the asceticism of those insular monks reminds us that there is no discipleship which does not demand a decision about our lifestyle, and a willingness to strive after the good. The sacramental world was seen by those saints in the Celtic lands as calling Christians to journey with the tension between the now and the not-yet. Recalling that view reminds us today that such a tension is still part of the Christian path.

3. LIVING ON THE FRINGES

God has indeed conferred this not insignificant grace on
[Columba] of blessed memory: that his name has gone
forth with fame not only to our own island of Ireland but
throughout the whole of Britain which is the largest of
the world's islands. Although he lived on this tiny island
out at the extremity of the Ocean near Britain, his renown
has spread to as far as three-cornered Spain and Gaul,
and then beyond the Alps into Italy, and has even reached
the head of all the cities: the city of Rome itself. This great
honour and fame was bestowed upon [Columba], along
with many other gifts, by God who loves, glorifies and
elevates to sublime honours those who love him and glorify
him with sweet praises. And blessed is He forever. Amen.

(Adomnán, *Vita Columbae* 3.23)

REMOTE PLACES

In the first chapter I argued that spirituality is always
embedded in a place, within a culture and its hopes, fears
and expectations. In the last chapter we examined how Celtic
Christians approached the creation around them as the
expression of God's love towards them and as a 'book' in which
they could 'read' of his nature and power. But how did they see
themselves, their place in the world and their place in history?

Adomnán's final comment in his *Vita Columbae*, quoted
above, can be seen simply as his exaggeration of the significance of his 'own' saint and predecessor as abbot of Iona,
whereby he finished his *Vita* with a comment similar to that

with which Athanasius closed his *Vita* of Antony. But it also tells us a lot about how the monks of Iona saw their place in the world. What strikes us at once is his sense of his own remoteness, out on the very edges of the land, perched on an island in the Ocean – that great mass of water that for Adomnán covered more than half the globe and lapped around the outer edges of the tripartite landmass of Europe, Asia and Africa. Humanity had spread outwards with the descendants of the son of Noah (Genesis 10) and they were in the last inhabited places. Still today we can feel that remoteness when we visit the Hebrides, 'The loneliest place on earth' said the composer Mendelssohn in the nineteenth century. But Adomnán's sense of remoteness was not just our sense of being 'far from the madding crowd' but that he was among those on the periphery of the Christian world. He felt part of the whole of Christendom, but on its edge. And part of seeing oneself on the edge is the need to shout out one's identity, telling those closer in not to forget those on the fringe.

Adomnán's contrast of Iona and Rome reveals both his sense of belonging as much as his sense of being remote. He is not struck by his remoteness as such, nor by its quiet and calm which any valley in the period could supply, but that Columba was so great a holy man that his fame could reach to the hub of things from the edge. People who live at the heart of affairs have a tendency to forget those out in the surrounding land. Geographers know that people who live near the centre of cities find it far more difficult to imagine a trip 'out' to the suburbs, than to imagine a trip 'in' towards the centre by those 'out there'. Similarly, those on the edge are pleased if they can claim the attention of those in the great metropolis. These are the feelings that Adomnán is dealing with: we know we are out here and have to clamour to be remembered, but now we have produced a man of God such that he can compare with the best of the more famous places, even Rome itself! Columba is like one of the preachers Paul speaks about in Romans 10: have the people not heard the gospel? 'Indeed they have; for "Their voice has gone out to all the earth, and their words to the ends of the world"' (Romans 10:18, citing Psalm 19:4). Columba has been one of those who have done the Lord's will; he has preached the gospel at the ends of the earth, and now his name is known throughout it.

In many texts from the Celtic lands there is a similar note of exaggeration. Muirchú, who wrote a *Vita* of Patrick towards the end of the seventh century, imagines the conversion of Ireland in Easter Vigil great drama, with the pagan king living in a splendid city like the Persian emperor; while other texts speak of the whole world bearing witness to the deeds of local saints. To these people on the periphery the exaggeration of their contribution to the whole becomes the necessary cry to show that even out there, there is life. Understatement seems to be the prerogative of those who live close to where their society believes 'it all happens'. Everyone on Iona had heard of Rome, but how many in Rome had heard of Iona? Adomnán wants to say that the local saint has done well, for he at least is known. Adomnán seems to have a similar attitude to his own place and culture – simultaneously proud of it, yet embarrassed that it is 'only a local' culture – to many African Christians today when they look at Europe: a strong desire to show that one is really as good as the churchpeople from the more 'famous' places. Adomnán knows that Christianity, books, splendid vestments and important news all come from the Continent; now, through the spread of Columba's fame, the traffic is no longer just one way.

Today Adomnán's sense of belonging seems strange, for we have to seek to avoid being absorbed into a vast global monotonous culture. Adomnán sees his relationship, he at the edge with Rome in the centre, without this threatening aspect. He wants to belong, he wants his saint recognised not just in the small body of those who are part of his monastery, but by the whole Body of Christ. Rome and Iona are not opponents, for each defines the other. Iona is the remote outpost (as far to the north-west as one could go on 'the orb of the lands') because it is so far from Rome; Rome is the 'head' because everywhere else looks to it. Adomnán perceived the inhabi-

tants of both places as united in the great enterprise of being
the People of God – the people who have inherited all that God
promised to those who love him.

Adomnán elsewhere shows that he has a sense of belonging
to three different communities: he belongs to the Irish, and he
can distinguish this cultural group from that of the Picts –
another Celtic people then inhabiting much of the area of
present-day Scotland – and from the Anglo-Saxons. Second,
he belongs to the Christian people through baptism and this
gives him an identity more basic and far-ranging than any
other: it links him with the people of Palestine and Egypt,
Constantinople and Sicily, Spain and France, and Italy and
Rome. Together they can be distinguished from pagans and
Jews and, possibly, Muslims. (Adomnán was the first Latin
writer to comment on the Muslim control of the Holy Places.
It is not clear whether he recognised them as a different
religion, or simply as a different race.) He saw the Christians
as a single body, with Christ as its head. As such they were
unified as any tribe or race is unified, for they had one origin
(Jesus) in the way that an Irish tribe had a single ancestor,
and so they were his sons and daughters; they had one lord to
whom they now looked – Jesus the Christ, guiding them from
heaven. Third, Adomnán belonged to a particular family, the
sons/disciples of Columba, among whom he would pass his life
for that was God's will. Among them he would die and be
buried in the same land. It would be with them that he would
await the Last Day in his grave: 'for the hour is coming when
all who are in the tombs will hear his voice and come forth,
those who have done good, to the resurrection of life, and those
who have done evil, to the resurrection of judgement' (John
5:28–29).

Today when we hear scriptural passages in the liturgy, either
about the tribal wars in Kings or any of the descriptions of
tombs in which a patriarch was buried – or worse when we
hear any of the genealogical passages – we may become exas-
perated that 'such stuff' is greeted as the Word of God. But to
Adomnán these were among the parts of the Scriptures that

spoke most directly to him and his people. He knew tribal warfare at first hand – it was endemic in his society and he expended much effort in trying to mitigate its suffering. And, just as the scriptural writers assumed that God took sides in this so that 'his people' either triumphed or were punished for their sins by defeat, he assumed that God could take sides and manifest his will in these matters. Conscious that he was Irish and a member of a family that could be related to a common ancestor, all the genealogical material in Scripture was inherently interesting to Adomnán. He knew himself as a member of the Cenél Conaill – the ruling family in the northern part of Ireland – which was also the family of Columba and the five other abbots before him, and we can still construct his family tree! His own culture shared many of the values of those who originally compiled that material, and just as biblical writers created genealogies to forge alliances between groups, so Adomnán looked to those lists of ancestors to find his people's relationships to the rest of humanity. By tracing an ancestry back to the Flood the Irish became part of the whole history of God's providence, and then it was simply a matter of location that they were among the last peoples to hear the gospel. God's people were those alive now, those who would hear the gospel in the future, and those who had died and who were now waiting for resurrection – the community was always larger than the visible group. Christ had begun the liberation of the tombs by leaving his own, and had promised to visit Adam and call to him: 'Awake, O sleeper, and arise from the dead, and Christ shall give you light' (Ephesians 5:14), and so this was also Christ's own destiny. Columba had indicated to a young monk that his true monastic home would be where he should eventually be buried to await the resurrection (*Vita* 2.39), and so even if he did live in a remote place – far from the great centres of Jerusalem, Alexandria, Constantinople and Rome – that was still the place to which God had called him and it would be from there he would greet the Lord at the End. Can we delve more deeply into this sense of being appointed to live in a time and place?

PATRICK: AT THE ENDS OF THE EARTH

The Christian sense of the spreading out of Christianity results in large measure from the way Luke at the end of his Gospel and the beginning of Acts imagines the gospel moving outwards from Jerusalem. Those who follow him are to be his 'witnesses in Jerusalem and in all Judea and Samaria and to the ends of the earth' (Acts 1:8). The gospel will spread out in concentric circles from Jerusalem, to the surrounding area of the Holy Land, and then out to the nations until it reaches 'the ends of the earth'. Jerusalem is the 'mother' (Galatians 4:26; Matthews 23:37) from whom the missionaries go out, and Jerusalem will be the final gathering place. The people beyond the boundary of the Holy Land are seen as grouped in 'nations' and the preaching moves on to nation after nation. We see this in Paul, for the mystery 'is made known to all nations' (Romans 16:26) and in the command 'to teach all nations' (Matthew 28:19). This notion of many nations hearing the law (Micah 4:2) continued as a theme in the Church as we see from this slogan: 'Great indeed, we confess, is the mystery of our religion: He was manifested in the flesh, vindicated in the Spirit, seen by angels, preached among the nations, believed on in the world, taken up in glory' (1 Timothy 3:16). It is with this background that we should imagine Patrick setting about his task of preaching, and in a similar vein his hearers fitting the new religion into their existing culture.

Patrick was keenly aware of his own origins among small-time Roman colonial gentry, with clergy among them, and that he was an alien in Ireland. He expresses some of the classic symptoms of homesickness, imagining what he could do if back among those who would understand him, and angry that they did not appreciate his suffering in remaining in Ireland. But he must stay in Ireland as it is the last nation to hear the gospel which he, Patrick, must bring to it. The task begun at Pentecost in Jerusalem, which entered Europe when Paul responded to a vision of a Macedonian calling him to preach in Greece (Acts 16:9–10), finally reached 'the ends of the earth' with a man in a vision calling Patrick over from Britain to preach in Ireland. Patrick was with the last nation to hear the gospel, at the very edge, and so he saw himself as the last apostle. He was there not because he liked it, but in obedience to the will of God. This was the place Patrick had to be in order to fulfil the vast divine plan, and he had to stay there until death.

This notion of a 'nation' (*gens*) hearing the Word became an enduring theme in insular writing not only among the Celtic peoples, but was transmitted by them to the Anglo-Saxons and can be seen in Bede. If they are the last nation to hear the gospel at the earth's end, then it is the will of God that they are a 'nation'. They are not just there by accident, they are placed there by Providence and have their own special place in the history of salvation. As a nation they have been chosen, and stand in relation to the gospel in exactly the same manner as the nations whose conversion is described in Acts. Their own cultural reality was not seen by them as submerged into 'Christendom', rather they now stood among the People of God as a nation. This perception of Christianity as the gospel spreading through nation after nation goes along way towards explaining why we do not have extensive evidence for clashes between the old and new religions, indeed the transition appears as one of harmonisation rather than of confrontation. This is so much at odds with what we have seen of the work of missionaries in recent centuries that we find it hard to imagine the arrival of Christianity as anything other than the destruction of local consciousness through the importation of a foreign cult. It could, however, be that these converted nations actually had an increased sense of nationality through receiving Christianity. The new religion told them that they were not just a group of families but that larger biblical unity of a nation, and as such had a distinct place in relation to all the other nations on earth, even in God's plan for the whole creation. Then they could look back and see that they could fit not only their present but also their past into that history of God's plan of salvation.

AT THE EDGE OF TIME

About a century ago Albert Schweitzer proposed that a characteristic of the first Christians was an expectation that the
Second Coming was imminent. He argued that this could
explain their attitudes to marriage in 1 Corinthians 7:25–35:
'I mean . . . the appointed time has grown very short; from now
on, let those who have wives live as though they had none . . .
for the form of this world is passing away.' When the End did
not come, Paul had to develop a new approach. In later times,
there were various forms of millenarianism proposing that the
great apocalyptic judgement was either about to take place or
at a fixed point in the near future. None of these views was ever
dominant among Christians, and millenarianism was, from
the later second century onwards, marginalised in Christianity
and has since then only erupted either in times of great crisis
(for instance during the Black Death) or among sects that
define themselves against the majority of Christians. However,
it is clear that for anyone who does believe that 'the End is
nigh' this belief will have a major impact on how they live
their Christianity – in fact, it can become a defining feature
of their spirituality. We find a similar urgency about the End
in insular writings, which we must distinguish from any form
of millenarianism.

Patrick saw himself as the counterpart of Paul: Paul was
the first to preach to the nations, he was the last. But Patrick
also had a unique sense of urgency based on a belief that he
was the eschatological apostle – when he finished his allotted
task, then the End could come. This was not based on a special
revelation nor upon the theme that God would now execute
his judgement on the unrighteous – the classic sources of
apocalypticism – but on his view of God's plan for the gospel.
The plan was that all nations should hear of the Christ, and
this took all the time from Pentecost until his arrival in
Ireland. Likewise, Jesus has said that 'truly, I say to you, you
will not have gone through all the towns of Israel, before the
Son of man comes' (Matthew 10:23). So the length of the

world's duration was circumscribed by the task of letting everyone hear the gospel, and when that was almost finished the End would come. Patrick saw himself as finishing the job of proclamation, fulfilling his urgent task, and so then there would be no reason for the world to continue: the 'mystery hidden for ages' (Ephesians 3:9; Colossians 1:26) was now plain to all.

Patrick saw himself not only as a key figure in the apostolic task begun by the Spirit, but as the final witness whose work – as soon as he could bring it near completion – would usher in the return of Christ. For most of us today, if we heard of someone with a belief that he or she had been given such a task by God we would be both sceptical and affronted by their arrogance. The prayer of J. H. Newman that 'God has created me to do Him some definite service; He has committed some work to me which he has not committed to another. I have my mission' is made bearable only by the next line: 'I may never know it in this life.' Many of us even find the language of a programming Providence problematic and seek to express our notion of a Christian purpose in other terms, while we have learned to suspect as dangerous anyone who links his or her 'mission' with the final times. However, such criticisms of Patrick would be wholly misplaced: his sense of his task was not that of a psychologically disturbed person, but a simple deduction from the facts of history and geography known to him. The gospel's task would be finished with the nation at the ends of the earth – now it was happening. The task had been given to him, he had not asked for it. And so recognising the locality where he had to preach, he recognised that it was a task of particular significance, and that any delay he might cause by slacking was holding up the whole onwards movement of the creation.

We do not know if Patrick ever realised that the End was not an automatic consequence of his work. However, while his logic did not remain a feature among subsequent generations of Christians in the Celtic lands, a sense of appointment and that they were living in the final times did. Today, phrases which claim 'by divine appointment' – such as 'DG' on British coins – are seen as simply pompous relics of yesteryear. When we still see echoes of it in religion, especially when it is people in power claiming their position by God's deliberate choice, we feel affronted. However, the sense that one was put in a place and given a particular task and status was central to the notion of vocation among the Christian Celts; not to accept that placement was a basic disobedience. Whether it was the siting of the monastery, who was to be abbot, or who was to be admitted and where, all these were decisions outside of human choice. God's will also entered into the choice of kings, the ownership of land, the results of warfare and the outcome of sickness. The human task – and a key task of the holy man or woman – was one of discerning those decisions of God and so communicating the divine will. The role of human freedom lay in the need to accept that will, and in the reality of sin: if one disobeyed, one could be held responsible. Here also lay the importance of intercessory prayer: it sought to appeal directly to God so that in the contingent matters of this world he would, because of his mercy and love, elect one course rather than another. And here too the holy man or woman had a role, for his or her intimacy with God sprung from the ability to gain the divine 'ear' and ask for a particular outcome.

While later Christians in the Celtic lands did not follow Patrick in viewing the End as imminent, they did believe they were living in the final times. This is what Adomnán wrote in the preface to his *Vita Columbae*: 'In these final times of the earth, [Columba's] name shall be a light to the oceanic island-provinces.' Slightly later an anonymous Irish preacher wrote: 'Our Lord Jesus Christ has announced this to us ... that the end of this world is coming closer every day ... I hope his coming will be in the very near future and that he will judge the whole universe with fire' (*In nomine Dei summi*, homily 2). This is an alien notion to Christians today, for we think of time as just rolling on, day after day, and while we may measure time as 'AD' all this means is that we are using a Christian (or convenient) reckoning system; we no longer place the emphasis where these Celtic writers did, on 'the year *of the Lord*'.

By the seventh century when the great monasteries of Clonard, Bangor, Clonmacnoise and Iona were producing the Latin writers upon whose works the fame of the insular church rests, the view of history established, in the main, by Augustine was ubiquitous. Basing himself on the arithmetic of Matthew 1:17, Augustine saw the whole of history from Adam to Christ as a succession of five 'ages'. Each age was characterised by, first, a certain amount of divine knowledge through revelation, and, second, a certain quality of covenant relationship between God and his chosen people. Each age prepared for the next stage, and built upon the previous age, until they reached the crescendo, the birth of Christ. This was not the middle point of history (as we sometimes think of it by comparing 'Before Christ' with *Anno Domini*), but the climax of revelation and divine commitment towards which all previous history was leading. Every human being, as they expressed it each day in the eucharistic liturgy, was living in the final time of the 'new and eternal covenant' (cf. Luke 22:20). This final, sixth, age in which they were living was qualitatively different from those that went before. Now the whole plan of God was revealed, and they were tottering on the brink of the next stage, beyond the ages, the eternal life of heaven. They perceived themselves to be in the final act of a six-part drama, and the final act had already been running for 600 or 700 or 800 years – it seemed a long finale. In contrast to Greek Chiliasts at the time and later western millenarians, Celtic Christians did *not* speculate about numbers, for that was knowledge that belonged only to the Father, as Jesus had said: 'it is not for you to know times or seasons which the Father has fixed by his own authority' (Acts 1:7). However, each earlier age had not just to wait for days and years, but whole stages (or at least one stage) of creation's history to pass before humanity would reach the edge of time. For Christians the very next step in world history would be the end of time. So why wait or delay – this was the Lord's business. If eternity was the next stage, then why not anticipate it? Why not bring the desired conclusion that bit closer? Here lies part of the explanation for the attractiveness of the monastery. Here lies the root of their denigration of marriage in contrast to virginity in exegesis and canon law, the explanation of how they read texts like 1 Corinthians 7, and their criticisms of those who seemed too closely concerned with the creation 'for the form of this world is passing away' (1 Corinthians 7:31) and they would soon be with, and resemble, the angels, 'for in the resurrection they neither marry nor are given in marriage' (Matthew 22:30).

Some religious groups today predict the End as the final catastrophe, God meting out retribution, but this is not the notion of those ancient Celtic writers; for them the End was consummation, resurrection, glory, arrival and reality after image. It was the glory that beckoned them to live 'under the shadow of eternity'. Other – more mainstream – religious groups still use this rhetoric of eschatology today, but it rings hollow for we have abandoned the time-frame that gave it meaning. For example, officials in the Roman Catholic Church speak of vowed virginity and of clerical celibacy as 'eschatological witness', but in holding to that rhetoric – ignoring the incredulity of those who hear it – they fail to note that the view of time/eternity which produced that rhetoric has wholly disappeared! Perhaps one of the great benefits of reflecting on the spiritualities from the early Middle Ages, such as those of the Celtic lands, is that it throws into relief the question of how we see ourselves in time, and how our spiritual priorities are related to that perception.

NON-URBAN, NON-IMPERIAL

The sense of being on the fringe was also present among the Christians of the islands in that they were aware of how different their environment was to that both of continental Christians at the time and the believers they met in the Scriptures. In texts like the Book of Daniel they read of magnificent cities and splendid courts. In Augustine and Orosius they read the history of the empires of Greece and Rome, their schools of learning, and their vast literatures. Most of their Christian texts were from that imperial, urban environment. Yet much of the Celtic lands were outside that empire, and even those parts of Britain that were not taken under Anglo-Saxon control could only remember the time before the legions left (AD 410) as past splendour. Equally, when they encountered the Christian texts they met them in Latin, a language that was not their own. The Celtic peoples were among the first groups in the West to accept Christianity in a language that was not, at the very least, a *lingua franca*. In this they would anticipate many others (Angles, Saxons, Visigoths, Franks, Lombards and many other Germanic peoples) for whom the language of Christianity, its books and core liturgy, would have to be learned as a foreign tongue.

When we contrast the experience of someone like Eucherius in Lyons reading the Scriptures with that of someone in Ireland a few generations later, we see a massive cultural shift. Eucherius lived in a great city, Lyons, in the same empire within which Jesus had lived; he had Greek contacts around him, and even when he read the Scriptures in translation it was in his own language, Latin. A story of Christ going to the city of Jerusalem, its great temple, and being tried by the governor was all firmly within his own world. The Christian in Ireland fifty years later had not seen a city, had to learn a foreign language to read, and had to imagine the event by analogy with his surroundings. While he may have had a store of local religious traditions, customs and laws, and a body of history, this did not come with the dignity of writing to support it, and the process of rendering his own speech in writing was just beginning. In this he anticipated many Christians who would hear the gospel in centuries to come, and like those later people he probably felt that he was the poor man at the feast.

This sense of being culturally on the fringe gives all the writings of these Celtic Christians a certain piquancy: they wish to present themselves as having a culture equal to that which they meet, but let slip their sense that they do not match it by adopting images from Christianity to describe their own past. Muirchú, whose *Vita* of Patrick is theologically sophisticated, exemplifies this sense of being on the fringe. He wants to present Ireland meeting Christianity as a meeting of equals, but for a suitably august description of the native king he takes images from the Book of Daniel not his own experience; his 'capital city' is Tara and he has the style of 'emperor of the barbarians'.

The insular Christians knew that they were fully part of Christ through baptism, yet that culturally they were 'new-comers' from outside. Hence one quality of their spirituality is the tension arising from the need they felt to prove their credentials by stressing just how well they appreciated Christian culture. But that is balanced by the fact that being new to Christianity they could look at problems with fresh eyes – the most stunning example being their extension of a monastic model of spiritual therapy to cover all sin, thereby breaking the pastoral impasse that had baffled the great Latin fathers such as Augustine. But the price of fresh eyes was an awareness of their marginality.

BETWIXT HEAVEN AND HELL

This chapter began by citing Adomnán's *Vita Columbae*; a fitting end would be to note the structure of his even greater work *De locis sanctis*. Essentially, it is a guide to the holy places that his monks heard about in the Scriptures. The work begins with a description of the gates of Jerusalem which is on the fringe of heaven (Genesis 28:17 and Revelation 3:12), and closes with a description of the gates of hell (cf. Matthew 16:18), which he believed were just north of Sicily. His readers understood travel. Daily they went back and forth among the islands of the Hebrides, or further afield to Ireland or Lindisfarne or Jarrow, moving round the fringes of the world. But they also knew they were hovering in every movement of their lives on the fringe between time and eternity, seeking to live in the holy land of the saints that fringed heaven, while renouncing that which would draw them toward 'the second death, the lake of fire' (Revelation 20:14).

4. GOD BEYOND

As it is written, 'What no eye has seen, nor ear heard, nor the heart of man conceived, what God has prepared for those who love him'.
(A saying from a lost Jewish apocalypse cited by Paul as Scripture in 1 Corinthians 2:9)

STRIKING A BALANCE

We have been looking at how a profound sense that the universe points towards the world-to-come was a core element in the way that early medieval Christians viewed themselves, the material world, their place in history, and God. We have noted how that world-view was combined with a monastic asceticism which gave a special flavour to the spirituality of those who lived in the Celtic lands on this world's fringe. For Christians, however, all sacramental approaches to the mystery of God must be balanced by an awareness of the divine transcendence. There must be an acknowledgement that God is beyond words, images, number, limitation, and being such as we possess.

We depend on God absolutely, but his act of creating is without any necessity, it is a simple and free expression of his love. Without such a balance, sacramentalism runs many risks which can undermine the most basic of Christian beliefs. The most obvious and most frequently encountered problem is that of valuing the signs as if they were equivalent to God. This occurs when the signs are revered in a superstitious way as if they had an intrinsic holiness. Another risk of sacramentalism is that of imagining God as the immeasurable thick end of the wedge whose near edge is the earthly token, and so placing him in the same order of reality as ourselves. These dangers are not simply theoretical, they have been manifested again and again in the history of Christian belief and worship. Indeed we can see them in several aspects of contemporary Christianity. For many Catholics interest in the 'real presence' in the eucharistic elements can become such a focus that they forget that the Eucharist is only a sacrament, and not Jesus himself. Equally, among many Evangelicals there is such a devotion to 'the Bible' that they confuse the book with God's revelation, forgetting that it only records pointers given in this world. Again, among many Christians looking for an 'experience of God', this experience is the valued object rather than the relationship which might be opened up within such an experience. So an obvious question we must ask is whether there was any awareness of a need to have a corresponding presentation of the divine transcendence in the thought and liturgy of the Celtic lands in the first millennium. Put another way, have we any inkling that they realised that the Christian must journey on the very edge of human understanding, and recognise that his or her final destination is still beyond what can be imagined?

'INACCESSIBLE LIGHT': ERIUGENA

The obvious place to begin answering that question is with Eriugena (d. 877) who was the outstanding western theologian emphasising the 'unknowableness' of God in the early Middle Ages. Christened 'John' by his parents, he gained the designation 'Scottus' ('the Irishman') sometime after his arrival on the Continent as a teacher (probably towards the middle of the ninth century), and gave himself the sobriquet 'Eriugena' ('born of Ireland') – modelled on Virgil's *Graiugena* ('born of Greece') – by combining its 'born of' element with the Irish word for Ireland, *Ériu*. Eriugena produced the most distinctive systematic theology between Augustine and Aquinas, building upon two foundations: first, Augustine from whom he took over an elaborate sacramentalism, and second, works of Greek theologians which had not hitherto been used in the West, such as those of Gregory of Nyssa (330–395) and the pseudo-Dionysius (c. 500), from whom he received a tradition of negative theology stressing that God is unknown.

The image that Eriugena uses on several occasions is that from 1 Timothy 6:16, of God 'who alone has immortality and dwells in inaccessible light, whom none has ever seen or can see'. While Eriugena considers the knowable universe, the creation from the angels to earth beneath his feet, as coming forth from God, telling of its origin sacramentally, and returning to God, this is balanced by the transcendence of the Trinity beyond, beyond, beyond. Human destiny shall rejoice in the face that God will present to us, when we shall be deified by God sharing his life with us through and through, but the 'inner life' of God will always be infinitely greater than us, beyond all our capacity – for we are most essentially creatures.

This negative theology of Eriugena has been the subject of many studies in recent decades, mainly by those whose primary interest has been in his relationship to Platonic philosophy. Hence they have not emphasised the fact that in Eriugena this negative approach to God assumes that the reader already knows the sacramental approach of reading the universe like a book. We see this in the opening exchange between the teacher and the pupil in his masterpiece, the *Periphyseon*. The master (called by Eriugena *Nutritor* – 'one who nourishes') tells the pupil (*Alumnus* – 'one who is fed') that he wants an overview of 'the things which can be grasped by the mind and those that lie beyond its grasp' and so can be divided into 'the things which are and the things which are not'. The teacher says that he needs a term to cover both categories in his discourse, and that he will call it 'nature' (Book 1, 441A). This was a singularly unhappy choice of word as it has produced confusion ever since among those who glance at Eriugena, and has even led to cries of 'pantheist' or 'panentheist' (originally as a slur, more recently as a selling-point). The mistake occurs in thinking that the word 'nature' is being used as a collective term to cover *everything* – in which case, as Eriugena develops his analysis, it would include God. *But that is not Eriugena's use.* For him it is simply a term relating to the whole range of our discourse. For when I say 'I cannot know God in himself', the fact of my speaking of the ineffability of God is itself part of my knowing, part of my speech and, indeed, part of my teaching. As Augustine had pointed out, when we say 'God is ineffable', we are in the paradoxical situation that we have truly said something about God!

When Eriugena then tells us, a few lines later, of the divisions humans can make regarding all they can discourse about ('nature') we have the perfect balance of the divine infinity with the creation which breaths forth his life:

> NUTRITOR: It is my opinion that there are four headings (*species*) into which our discourse (*natura*) . . . can be divided:
> first, that which creates and is not created;
> second, that which creates and is created;
> third, that which is created and does not create;
> fourth, that which is not created and does not create . . .
> ALUMNUS: You are surely correct . . .

This may seem typical of the neat way that medieval theologians made distinctions fit together like a jig-saw, each division related to the others by a particular type of opposition, but for us it is enough just to note its central message. The first division is God and the fourth is the mental concept of 'nothing'. Both are ungraspable, but in our perception they must be as far apart as possible. The fourth is unknowable because there is nothing to know; the first is unknowable for its being is so beyond us, so superabundant, that we cannot comprehend it. That Being is so wonderful that it is the source of all else that exists: the second and third divisions which equal the domain of the creation. But God is distinct from these second and third divisions in that while they are dependent on a creator (each is created), the first division is characterised by the lack of any dependency (that is, it differs from the second and third divisions as being 'not created'). The second and third divisions embrace the universe and constitute the realm of our knowledge: they are within our grasp and our information about them comes from our study of them, and our knowledge of their origins from knowing what is revealed about the creation. Hence, much of the *Periphyseon* is, in effect, a commentary on Genesis/creation – the second and third divisions come with the marks of their origin and with an internal dynamism pointing them upwards.

The work of Eriugena, partly because of the difficulties of its language and partly because user-friendly editions are still some way off, has remained a domain for the researches of theologians and philosophers, but it is clear that Eriugena approached his task within a spirit of reflection and prayer – a facet of his work that we see more clearly in his *Homily on the Prologue of St John*. There he sees the human soaring upwards in the universe to seek the Source of being and life. But even when borne aloft on mystical wings, God remains wrapped from sight in the splendour of glory. However, we can see Eriugena's sense of seeking God even in that passage just quoted. It is a little meditation on all that comes within the reflection of our minds. We are confronted with the contingency of our existence, with the absolute holiness of God; as created beings we exist at the divine behest and within the divine scheme. Eriugena appreciates that we are sacramental beings, but God, towards which all his creation points, is beyond that creation.

As he has often been described, Eriugena is 'the peak within the plain'. He has that mark of genius that prevents us simply explaining him by context, and he made, uniquely for the time, use of the apophatic writings of the East. So, does his work provide an indication that there was a more widespread awareness of the need to balance a sacramental view of the creation with an awareness of the awesome mystery of God? It is my belief that it does, for while his great system may be the peak, it did not emerge from a flat plain – there is other evidence from the Celtic lands that there was an awareness of the incomprehensibility of God. And, while it cannot be proven, it may have been contact with these less sophisticated expressions of the divine transcendence that first alerted Eriugena – while still a young man at home – to the themes he would explore as a master.

THE LITURGY OF INEFFABILITY

The Stowe Missal's date of writing – when the manuscript was produced, not the date of origin of any of its contents – can be put at some time between 790 and 820. It is unexceptional as a missal – the Roman Rite with odd bits and pieces added by its various owners over a long period of use – but it does represent the actual prayers in use in at least parts of Ireland in the early ninth century. However, it preserves one text which has not been found elsewhere in surviving liturgical books: a preface (the opening, and variable part, of the Eucharistic Prayer) which stresses the ineffability of God. Since there is no translation of the missal, here is the whole text:

> The Lord be with you . . .
> Life up your hearts . . .
> Let us give thanks to the Lord our God . . .
>
> Father, all powerful and ever-living God,
> we do well always and everywhere to give you thanks
> through Jesus Christ our Lord.
> You [O Father], with your only begotten Son and the
> Holy Spirit are God.
> [You are] God, one and immortal;
> [You are] God, incorruptible and unmoving;
> [You are] God, invisible and faithful;
> [You are] God, wonderful and worthy of praise;
> [You are] God, strong and worthy of honour;
> [You are] God, most high and magnificent;
> [You are] God, living and true;

[You are] God, wise and powerful;
[You are] God, holy and splendid;
[You are] God, great and good;
[You are] God, awesome and peace-loving;
[You are] God, beautiful and righteous;
[You are] God, pure and kind;
[You are] God, blessed and just;
[You are] God, tender and holy.

[You are] God, not in the singularity of one person, but
in the trinity of one substance.

We believe you;
We bless you;
We adore you;
and we praise your name forever more.

[We praise you] through [Christ] who is the salvation of
the universe;
through [Christ] who is the life of human beings;
through [Christ] who is the resurrection of the dead.

Through him the angels praise your majesty;
the dominations adore;
the powers of the heaven of heavens tremble;
the virtues and the blessed seraphim concelebrate in
exultation;
so grant, we pray you, that our voices may be admitted
to that chorus, in humble declaration of your glory, as
we say:

Before looking at this, a few comments help to set the context.
While this prayer survives only in this missal from Co. Dublin,
this does not mean that it originated with this missal nor,
indeed, that it had its origins anywhere in the Celtic lands.
However, that does not mean that it throws no light on the
spirituality of early Irish Christians. First, a missal normally
contains many prefaces for different occasions and seasons –
the Stowe Missal contains only this one (the missal exhibits

several other signs of being made to a limited budget) and therefore represents a deliberate choice by someone: if there is going to be just one preface available to the user of this missal, then it shall be this. Second, whether it was written in Ireland, France or northern Italy (the missal shows contacts with the local variations of text of these places) is irrelevant. What is important is that during its time of use – and the missal passed through the hands of several priests who used it in their ministry – it formed the spirituality of these communities. And, how many other groups heard this preface from other missals that have not survived?

The basic image of this, as with all other prefaces, is that of offering thanks to the Father through the mediation of the Son; thus Jesus Christ is the perfect sacrament of the Father. However, rather than base the reason for our thanksgiving upon some gift of God to us, its cause for praise is the excellence of God's nature. This is described both negatively – incorruptible, immortal, unmoving and invisible – and by way of eminence: he is the most high, the one worthy of all good attributes. The central dynamism of the prayer is that of the contrast of God and creation.

If we take the praises individually they are no more than the attributes that can be found used of God throughout the tradition, but the cumulative effect of listing, litany-fashion, thirty attributes is greater than the sum of its parts. The whole prayer presents a God who is radically 'other'. He is the living source of all else, the one who *is* all these attributes which in our experience are passing in creatures. He is the one we worship, and it is to the Father's court that we gain access through Christ. The worship of the earthly group is linked with ever more elevated choirs of angels until it joins with that of the seraphim – the highest of creatures but who have to cover themselves in the presence of God (Isaiah 6:2). A liturgy which had this prayer in its repertoire had a foil against the crasser dangers of sacramentalism, and a powerful reminder of the unique mediation of Christ – as they saw it in the letter to the Hebrews – in giving us access to the Father.

PICTURING CREATION

Eriugena was a single great scholar, but does he reflect the age? The preface we have just examined was used, but we do not know how widely. My third example is from a textbook for training priests: here we have the sort of work which can diffuse its vision widely. The work is known as the *Book on the Order of Creatures* (*Liber de ordine creaturarum*) and many scholars believe it was written in Ireland in the seventh century. Even if it was not composed there, it was certainly in widespread use there. It is a guide which seeks to present an orderly account of the whole creation based on the Genesis creation stories. Although virtually unstudied, it has the distinction of being one of the first systematic monographs on the creation written after the major Latin fathers. From chapter 2 onwards it moves through space, and then through time, to show that all things are created within an order and that God acts in a measured way in all his works. This takes concrete form in the text in its desire to record measurements, extents and weights so the reader may understand the creation and know the divine handiwork in detail. The account *descends* through the creation. The first (and the highest and least heavy) creatures are the ordered ranks of angels (the spiritual creatures); then the upper heavens; then the lower heavens; then the devil (this is the area of the universe between the earth and the lowest part of the heavens 'where they wander for the ruin of souls'); then earthly realities; then human beings; then beneath the surface of the earth; and finally, the future life of heaven.

Here is that pattern in skeletal form:

Chapter	The structure of the universe
2. Spiritual Creatures	The ordered ranks of the angels which form a hierarchy of spheres

3. The waters above the firmament	Outermost edge of material universe
4. The firmament	The outermost visible reality
5. Sun and Moon	The heavenly bodies
6. The upper regions and paradise	The sky in which the heavenly bodies move
7. The lower regions and the atmosphere	The region beneath the moon which is subject to change and the region in which the weather exists
8. The devil and the demons	The lowest regions of the atmosphere – the air we breath
9. Water and the ocean	Water's natural position is just below air
10. The paradise of Adam	This is the finest of earth (*terra*) and so should be just below water in the overall scheme
11. The terrestrial world	What we walk upon
12. Human nature	Humans
13. Sins and Punishment	The fiery places beneath the earth entered through special gates
14. The Fires of Purgatory	The very centre of the material universe
15. The future life	Beyond all material reality; back to the start.

Before all this is a praise of God in chapter 1: while the creation can be described, that cannot be attempted with God – the student must simply praise the Trinity. Moreover, the praise in this first chapter, 'On faith in the Trinity', is expressed in terms of it being the negation/opposite of created reality. In a manner that seems to anticipate Eriugena, the book opens: 'Everything that is within our minds ought to be seen to admit one major distinction: between focusing on God and things; or put another way, we can distinguish between Creator and creatures.' That opening line establishes the key distinction: God is not a creature, not a thing, nor the highest element in a scale that reaches upwards. It then proceeds with a long list pointing out that God is, for example, beyond number, location, need and every other limitation. He is goodness without quali-fication, greatness without quantity, and eternity without time. He cannot be grasped by the creature nor comprehended by the intellect. The balance is as perfect as with Eriugena, if expressed in a more accessible language: one must study the creation and see God's marks in order, number and weight; but the Lord himself, Father, Son, Spirit, is wholly other, an infinity, and all else depends upon his creative 'let it exist'.

DOING THE NUMBERS

For many people today one of the most tiresome features of the writings of the insular world is their fascination with numbers, and above all with getting the right date for Easter. This interest is directly related to their belief that God has given order to his creation; it is a beautiful work, and it must be capable of being expressed in numbers. However, whenever we find people who use numbers in relation to religion we have a vantage point from which to observe how those people view God. For the classical pagan world into which Christianity was introduced there was a common question, 'How many gods are there?' Then the answer could range from zero (the atheist), or one (certain philosophies), to many (various religions), or uncertainty (agnostics). The basic notion is that whatever a supreme being would be, one could tick its existence as either there or not in a manner analogous to going through a ship's manifest. However, for Jews and Christians, the object of our worship, from whom we receive being, is true infinity: to ask the question 'How many?' is blasphemous. We do not believe that there is 'one god', but that 'God is one' (Deuteronomy 6:4/ Mark 12:29). Hence, number is something that belongs to the creation; God as infinite Being can never be the subject of any numbering.

This has been a very hard lesson for Christians to learn. The old pagan attitude just keeps popping up in its simple form by contrasting other religions with Christianity on the basis of whether or not 'they have got to a belief in one god' – that is a meaningless comparison if it just means they believe there is a single, trans-material source of power. Another form of this temptation to think that God can be numbered appears when Christians overdo it with regard to the mystery of the Trinity, and one gets games of three-in-one and one-in-three as if the mystery were a mathematical conundrum that could be sketched out on paper with triangles – the pious equivalent of finding the Fermat's Last Theorem. Given that Christians in the Celtic lands were still close to their pre-Christian culture, and that they received Christianity with this interest in the numbered order of the creation, it would not be surprising if we found such a confusion. The amazing thing is that we do not: their scriptural commentaries – which are full of counting this and that – make it crystal clear that God is beyond number. Number, in all its grades, including one, is found only in creatures. The numbers found in creation point to the one who is beyond number, beyond understanding and the limitations implied in number and understanding.

If that is the case, why has St Patrick has been linked with a shamrock as if he would try to teach the nature of God with the arithmetic game? And why do many modern studies explain every occurrence of a decoration with three elements as 'trinitarian'? Both are later impositions from cultures theologically far less literate and astute than that which they seek to explain.

THE UNENDING JOURNEY

Augustine lifted his gaze higher and higher in the creation and was told by the whole of that creation that God was still higher and beyond. This has become the theological touchstone of 'God is ever greater' (*deus semper maior*). In effect it means that the Christian must live with an incomplete understanding: the journey never ends, it goes to the very edges of language and understanding, and it is still only beginning.

It might be objected that the concern with the otherness of the Creator is a crucial point of doctrine and theology but has little impact on spirituality – it seems an obscure matter and remote from how a Christian lives her or his life. Experience tells a different story! Whenever Creator and creation are placed on the same plane in the imagination, the creation becomes filled with absolutes: God becomes a tyrant pulling all the strings, and indeed we start considering our relationship with God in terms of a 'Boss' on the good days and a prison governor on the bad days. If, however, the notion enters our consciousness that there is complete dependence of the creation on the Creator, without any reciprocal need in the Creator for the creation, then how we view life and all around us changes utterly. This was the great discovery of Basil the Great (330–379), Ambrose of Milan (339–397) and Augustine (354–430), and from them it became the common possession of western Christians in the early Middle Ages.

The most immediate consequence is that it allows one to see *all as gift*. Everything we have is there by God's will, and when we are struck by its sheer givenness, we become aware in a new way of the beauty around us, and almost at once we become more keenly aware of the goodness of God. To appreciate that all is gift is a complex sensation. At once the universe is more valuable, for it is not 'just there', but there because God wants it to be, and so it is more fragile and more valuable. But being there as gift, it is also passing and dependent, transient and needy; and reflection upon it leads to both praise/thanks and petition/lament – and indeed the consciousness that, as a modern preface reminds us, 'the desire to thank you is itself your gift'. We see this realisation in many of the prayers and writings that have survived from insular sources.

This awareness of the giftedness of creation is central to

living with the tension that material things must be valued, that Christians must work in the world now to improve it. For they do not just happen to be there, they are there by a choice of God's love. At the same time they know that it is but a shadow, and nothing in comparison with the reality of God. Hence when early medieval writers, such as those who compiled the Penitentials, contrast the physical and the spiritual, they are not using our distinction of matter versus spirit which for many is equivalent to God/religion versus the world/ordinary life. To recognise the unique existence of God is to recognise that he is the creator of all: material things, spiritual realities, thoughts, forces in creation, and the angels. Now the dispute between spirit and matter has a completely different context – it is simply a dispute about shifts in emphasis to maximise the good. Thinking, or trying to think, of God not only as 'wholly other' but as the infinity from whom creation exists is the very antithesis of a materialism – that is a notion that scriptural commentators from the Celtic lands discuss as something almost beyond the imagination and belonging to the darkened minds of those who had not encountered Christ. Materialism sets physical existence as we experience it as the gauge of how real anything else is; upon this scale God has the least existence for we cannot touch, see or measure him. The exact opposite is the position of a universe that is simply a gift. No creature has existence in themselves, but only through dependence on the Creator, in need of God's creative love to hold it in existence; and matter has the least stable existence with the least potential. These are radically diverse viewpoints on the whole human endeavour. While many would reject materialism in its cruder forms, it is a powerful idea in our world not least among Christians who view matter as the gauge of reality or as possessing some indestructible capability to exist 'alongside' God. One of the valuable services of recalling this earlier spirituality is that it reminds us how such notions of matter jar with the Christian belief in a creator.

There is another, altogether more jolly, aspect to abandoning notions of some sort of 'eternal matter' and a 'supreme being' who then shapes it up, and replacing it with the perspective of God freely creating all that exists from his love: there is room for joy and freedom in the universe. To believe that God has freely created is to believe that we are in his hands, and that no matter how bad things look, then his reality still undergirds us, still supports us, and that full life is with him. It is from this perspective that earlier Christians read about being free from anxiety in Matthew 6:25–30: 'Consider the lilies of the field, how they grow; they neither toil nor spin . . . But if God so clothes the grass of the field, which today is alive and tomorrow is thrown into the oven, will he not much more clothe you, O men of little faith?' (vv. 28–30). It is this sense that they should be free from concerns, that God's power is caring for them, that gives so much of what these earlier Christians wrote a lightness and care-freeness that we find alternately attractive and annoying. It is also reflected in the playfulness that can be found in so much of their writing and art. If being and life are a gift which make sense solely in terms of their divine destiny when God will be all in all (cf. Ephesians 4:6), then the response of praising God and of spending resources in his service – be it the artwork of an illuminated manuscript, building chapels on craggy outcrops of rock, or making long journeys to seek wisdom or to preach – is not just a pious decision about resources and lifestyle, but a whole perspective on life that is coherent with one's most basic beliefs about all that exists.

Let me end this chapter with a more earthy speculation. Eriugena produced one of the masterpieces of western theology dealing with the incomprehensibility of God. Did he know the preface found in the Stowe Missal? Did he ever read the *Liber de ordine creaturarum*? He certainly could have attended a Eucharist at which the preface was used, for it was definitely being used in at least one missal at the time he was growing up. He may have read the *Liber* during his basic studies for it was being studied in Ireland at the time. We shall never be able to answer these questions precisely, but we can be sure of this: within his own religious background in the Celtic lands there was a formal theological awareness that the Source of Being must never be thought of in a similar way to the creation, can never be identified with the creation, and can be more truly thought of in terms of negations. It was perhaps this basic formation in faith that first sparked an interest that caught fire when Eriugena met the writings of Gregory of Nyssa, Maximus the Confessor (*c.* 580–662) and the pseudo-Dionysius.

5. JOURNEYS OF FAITH

> And holy man Patrick was called to leave the place that
> was bathed in light and come outside into the king's pres-
> ence – and the magi said to their own people: 'We must
> not rise when he comes among us, for whoever rises at his
> coming will later believe him and worship him!'
>
> (Muirchú, *Vita Patricii* 1.17)

In the first four chapters I have tried to introduce the spirituality of a distant time with broad strokes, and to identify the
basic architecture of that spirituality upon which its more
detailed aspects were built. In this chapter and the two following I want to look at how people in the Celtic lands
presented to themselves the challenges of being a disciple, one
who had entered the body of Christ in baptism. I want to
examine this in terms of three journeys: first, the whole of the
Christian life seen as a pilgrimage toward Christ; second, how
they conceived the journey back to the Christian Way for those
who having embarked on the Christian journey later found
themselves wandering in other directions; and last, how they
saw the life of journeying making demands on them in the
practical decisions of life.

In order to enter into the spirituality of another time and
culture one needs a common motif – some theme that *they
recognised* as providing a basic image for the Christian life,
but which *we also find relevant* as a metaphor for discipleship.
This is why I have opted for the notion of a *journey* as the
basic metaphor of the whole book, but in particular wish to
look at the topics of these three chapters as variants on that

motif. Insular Christians were very conscious that faith had travelled to them and that they had to travel as part of the demands of being Christians. They valued pilgrimage, and they were conscious of the imagery of the Christian life as a journey towards a homeland (cf. Hebrews 11:14): the heavenly Jerusalem. Today, many Christians no longer resonate with the older languages of Christianity which imagine being a Christian with static metaphors, such as holiness as 'a state of life'. We are ever more conscious of how our lives change and grow, that what seems a good way forward at one stage may later be constricting or unfulfilling, and that changes in life's circumstances are part of being human. Thus we find mobile images, such as 'following' or 'journey' or 'pilgrimage', useful, for these reflect our basic desires, intentions and the pursuit of a distant goal, while recognising that changes, side-adventures and the need to take round-about routes are always present in life and are not just interruptions. Both for ourselves and for those in the early insular world there is an awareness that movement lies at the very core of life. This feature not only connects us, but sets both ourselves and those earlier Christians apart from many of the scholastic and Reformation-inspired spiritualities where the status of the soul with regard to God was the central concern (for example, 'in sin', 'in grace', 'having sanctifying grace', 'being saved') and life's changes were seen as either peripheral to that status or something that was only to be considered in so far as it might be disruptive of an achieved state.

However, if we are to gain an insight into how earlier Christians conceived of the living of Christianity there are other criteria we have to keep in mind so that we are (as far as this is ever possible between long-separated periods) comparing like with like. Clearly, we must try to select materials that are broadly related in culture and date. The 'Celtic world' extended over at least half-a-dozen languages in two language families, each region had a different background and social forces at work in it. While the time span embraced by the term 'early medieval Christian Celtic' can be more than 600 years in duration. Items picked at random from across such a spread would not form a meaningful group for us to examine. Therefore all the materials shall come from just one culture, Ireland, from a period of just over a century, from the late seventh to the early ninth centuries. My choice is determined by the fact that this is the earliest place from which we can assemble a sufficiently large body of written material to assess their spirituality. Moreover, by selecting documents written in Latin we can be confident that here we have documents that were intended for a wide circulation and which saw themselves in dialogue with a broad Christian audience.

Given that my theme is journeys/pilgrimages, it may come as a surprise that I do not intend to examine the spirituality of those who went off to the Continent, leaving home behind them, either as penitents, missionaries or students. This group, the *peregrini*, of whom the most famous is Columbanus, who declared that they went abroad 'for the love of Christ', have become a stock element in books on 'Celtic spirituality' and 'the Irish and civilisation', but they tell us very little that is relevant to our purpose here. Those who left their country may have been the heroes of the time, and certainly they can be presented in a most vivid manner today – they are major players in the current mythology of the 'Celtic Church' – but they do not provide us with an insight into how ordinary men and women imagined their Christian life and sought 'to fight the good fight, to finish the race, to keep the faith' (cf. 2 Timothy 4:7). We need to listen to the kind of material that was delivered to people in the equivalent of the average 'parish church' to appreciate the spirituality of lay women and men, and to hear what was being held out as an ideal to the many monks who joined a nearby community and stayed there for the remainder of their lives (the number of monks in monasteries in Ireland always vastly outnumbered those who went far afield). In effect, this means we must pay attention to the stories, the handbooks of discipline such as the penitentials, and the sermons of those earlier times. This is not nearly as exciting as the accounts of Gall and Columbanus and Fursey, but it brings people more like ourselves into view who are still our brothers and sisters in the communion of Christ.

So what shall we use for an insight into how these Christians viewed the Christian life as a journey? The answer lies in listening to the stories they composed with the express intention of edifying an audience and provoking an imitation. I wish to take two of the best Christian stories that have survived from the period and look at them as deliberately composed myths that express what their authors believed was the central vision of Christian life. The first – which was written to appeal to a wide audience – is the *Vita Patricii* by Muirchú (late seventh century); the other, written with a specifically monastic audience in mind – but whose appeal as a story made it the medieval equivalent of a bestseller – is the anonymous *Nauigatio sancti Brendani* (probably early ninth century). If we can hear the lessons of those authors with their liturgical vision of the Christian life, we can begin to enter into their spiritual world.

LEGEND AND SPIRITUALITY

Before we look at the stories, there is a major obstacle: many will shout that 'those stories are bunkum!' The simple answer is that they are bunkum, if and only if the opening chapters of Genesis are bunkum. If you are a cosmologist and you read Genesis 1 as an account written with the intention of doing what you do, then it is nonsense; the same applies if you are a palaeontologist or archaeologist and you believe that Genesis 2 – 11 is an account of the origins and earliest history of the human race. In past times, indeed for most of Christian history, there was no need even to imagine such a distinction, but today we must see those early Hebrew documents, and the 'Book of Genesis' into which they were woven, as valuable for what they tell us about the religious imagination of those people, not as primitive attempts to do what we do in the mode of empirical science. Genesis is the work of the religious imagination, presenting a view of the cosmos as a creation, and an attempt to make sense of the human predicament. As such, it is a precious insight into our own religious history. The same is true in varying ways of the *Vita Patricii* and the *Nauigatio*: both present themselves as historical accounts, both have historical people as their central characters, and employ local colour for verisimilitude; but both are essentially imaginary in that the primary guide used by their authors is not what *has* happened, but what *should* happen in an ideal Christian world. Muirchú wants to present the ideal Christian, who is also the ideal missionary; while the author of the *Nauigatio* wants to present a picture of what the ideal monastery should be like. Both share the same central sources for their pictures: the Scriptures, the liturgy, other saints' lives, and monastic texts such as the writings of Cassian. Historical odds and ends, traditions that may or may not be historically true, are just worked into the tales and give them a flavour of the local scene.

Alas, the history of the interpretation of these tales exactly mirrors that of Genesis. Until the nineteenth century both were treated as 'history' without much ado: stories just accepted at face value in the same way that similar stories in the Scriptures were held as true. Then with the rise of critical history there were frantic efforts made by some to 'prove' they were historical in a manner similar to the desperate effort to try to 'reconcile' Genesis with science. Only in recent decades has the wise counsel of the great Jesuit scholar Hippolyte Delehaye, originally propounded at the beginning of the twentieth century, come to the fore: a saint's life tells us primarily about the time of its composition, not of the time it purports to narrate. This has been taken to heart by historians who examine Muirchú as a witness to ecclesiastical politics in the seventh century and the desires of a powerful dynasty, the Uí Néill, to establish their central religious site, Armagh, as the religious capital of Ireland. Only more slowly, however, has it been recognised that whatever its political agenda, Muirchú was also a theological writer presenting a view of the Christian life. It is this that we want to glimpse.

The problem is even more complicated with the *Nauigatio*. Since it speaks of meeting 'islands' off the coast of Ireland (they forget that on these 'islands' lived people like Judas Iscariot!), they become obsessed with the notion that it might be some folk memory of an ancient discovery of America! Indeed, there has been so much interest in these pseudo-historical questions and crazy 'experiments', like a voyage from Ireland to America in a skin boat 'to show it could be done', that people forget that the only destination actually mentioned is reached when those in the boat have learned to celebrate the perfect Liturgy of the Hours. We have to group all those 'experiments' about Brendan as a seaman with the similarly conceived 'trials' of the nineteenth-century biblicists who sought to construct Noah's ark so that it would fit the required number of animals and their feed, and agree with the dimensions given in Genesis 6:15. Both groups of 'experimenters' miss the point of the stories by not recognising that a fiction, a story, as narrative and drama, can perform the task of communicating the divine just as effectively, if not more so, than a systematic analysis.

It is worth noting that while we may think that the idea that one can communicate a spirituality in a good yarn is a modern one – we think of the Screwtape books of C. S. Lewis – or at best as old as John Bunyan's *Pilgrim's Progress* (1678–1684), throughout the history of Christianity there has been an awareness that the story can speak to the imagination more directly than formal analysis or religious admonition. The liturgy presents a history of humanity and vision of our end that is communicated in various dramas. The stories of Christmas and Easter are more important in Christian life than treatises on the incarnation or soteriology. The various legends – here used in a formal sense of stories of the saints that can be read – have inspired and encouraged and amused Christians. A modern counterpart might be *Star Trek*, which has often been seen as a sequence of secular parables. The religious tale, as I shall look at it here, is a finite image that is transparent, a window into a transfinite reality.

PATRICK'S JOURNEYS

Muirchú presents Patrick as the Christian holy man. He is the Christian writ large who met in his life in a spectacular fashion all that the ordinary Christian meets at a more humble and domestic level. He is someone who is called in a miraculous way to preach the gospel, who must fulfil its demands despite dangers, and who is presented so as to resemble the great holy men of Scripture and ultimately Christ himself. As regards historical sources, Muirchú had very little to go on: he had Patrick's own writings (or, at least, the *Confessio*); he had places that claimed contact with Patrick (already well known as 'the great missionary'); possibly some traditions deriving from the man himself; and an awareness that Patrick had succeeded. These, along with his understanding of what a saint should be, were enough to produce what he needed. It is his understanding of what a saint *should be* that we need to recover.

Muirchú tells us that Patrick had escaped from slavery in Ireland. Then he tells us of Patrick's many ups and downs before his return there at the moment of God's choosing. Now returned as an apostle, Patrick's first task is presented as going back to the man who held him as a slave. He must go to him to buy his own freedom from slavery, but also to liberate his former owner, Miliucc, with the faith of Christ. Miliucc, fearing the approach of Patrick and inspired by the devil, chose to destroy himself, his wealth and his house in fire. Patrick was stunned into silence and mourning at the event: that someone should choose death in fire rather than eternal life, a way of destruction without a future rather than a heavenly throne and future generations having a similar hope. Patrick is presented as the man upon whom the Lord's favour rests; yet confronted with the situation he expresses a lack of comprehension, using words (out of context) from Paul: 'I do not know, God knows' (2 Corinthians 12:2). Then Patrick blessed the area and left.

That an escaped slave should, out of justice, seek to pay for his freedom is an aspect of Christian preaching that is rightly foreign to us. It should not be forgotten that it was only in the nineteenth century that Christians, with a lot of hesitations, began to condemn slavery as morally wrong. For Muirchú the demands of natural commutative justice were primary – something that we preach when we speak of social injustice – and extended even to slaves with their masters. We are on less unfamiliar ground when we see another aspect of the story: the people we must be most anxious to bring to the life of faith are those who have hurt us most. Patrick's action is held as a model of forgiveness, of loving one's enemies and praying for those who persecute us (cf. Matthew 5:44). In this first incident in Ireland as a bishop, Patrick has been established as one who has mastered the central attitudes of Christian holiness.

The self-destruction of Miliucc is carefully presented as a result of his deliberate choice, and the whole incident works as an *exemplum* of a theme that goes back to the earliest Christian preaching: the 'two Ways'. The gospel's arrival presents the most stark of choices: a way that leads to a future or one that leads to total destruction. The future is not just eternal life and a throne in heaven for the individual, but one that brings with it the possibility of life for future generations, a destiny for a whole community; the individual's choice has effects far beyond their own lifetime on earth and these far-flung connections must impact on one's decision. To accept the gospel both brings life to oneself, and gives it to those who depend upon one.

In this little morality tale Muirchú shows insight into the human predicament: it is not a simple two-dimensional choice between 'the nice way' and 'the nasty way' in the manner of a children's story. There is something dark and incomprehensible about the way people react to the gospel. Muirchú presents Miliucc as fearful and antagonistic from the very first mention of Christianity in his area. He already fears the new religion – presumably as it could cause him harm – yet he then does something that is wholly irrational: he harms himself. Why does he do the very thing that brings about the destruction he so fears? Why does he prefer something so repulsive as his own death, and with it such wanton destruction, rather than the new faith? Why is it so difficult to opt for the Christian way with its benefits? Muirchú does not try to explain such human decisions, nor does he present Patrick as having the answers. The only explanation he offers is that pride prevents Miliucc meeting Patrick lest he be subject to his former slave, and, echoing John 13:27, that the devil entered his mind and tempted him. But still the choice of the way of death is inscrutable, and the Christian who sees such a self-destructive decision can, like Patrick, only sigh, weep, mourn and pray for the person. Yes, the Christian is offered two Ways in which to walk, one towards life and the other towards death, but the choosing in the concrete situations of life is by no means straightforward.

THE EASTER JOURNEY

For Muirchú the actual conversion of Ireland happens in a single night: that of the Easter Vigil. Just as the Vigil celebrates the deliverance of the people of Israel from slavery in Egypt through the Red Sea, the liberation of the Jews from having to worship idols in Babylon (Daniel 24), the liberation by the risen Christ of those waiting in chains in their tombs, and the baptism of Christians passing from death to life, so Muirchú creates a drama with the symbols of the Vigil liturgy, new fire, new light, extended so that it embraces the whole conversion of the island. The people of Ireland, so argues Muirchú, have passed from one kind of existence to another through believing in Jesus Christ, from the 'age of the law of nature' to the final 'age'. This in fact is his own understanding of what baptism – and all that is celebrated at the Easter Vigil – means in the life of a Christian. He writes about Ireland, but his premise is his understanding of baptism. By looking at what he says becoming Christian means for the island, we see how he actually understood baptism.

Having invoked the theme of the two Ways at the beginning

of the work, one might imagine that Muirchú would present the relationship of paganism to Christianity in the same manner: one being life, the other death. However, reality for him is far more complex. Already – before Patrick arrives – the Irish, as presented by Muirchú, have been prepared for the reception of the gospel through the invisible workings of the Holy Spirit who enlightens minds to the truth and who dispenses the gift of prophesy. Near the beginning of the *Vita* he departs from his storyline to let the readers know that the wise men (*magi*) of the Irish pagan religions knew that a new teaching would come among them, a religion of power that could overthrow kingdoms, and that will be the end of their power (I.11). The *magi* are imagined (with many scriptural echoes) as having a vast body of written wisdom which they can consult so as to discover a 'preparation for the gospel'. Then later Muirchú presents the meeting of the forces of the old and the new, and the new is presented as that which completes the people who until now have been deprived of the fullness of the truth. The relationship of paganism to Christianity is seen as one of anticipation and fulfilment: their own religion had prepared them for Christ, Patrick was the appointed minister who delivered Christ's life to them.

Muirchú saw the Christian life not as an imposition from outside the person, but that which brought the individual into harmony with divine providence. It was a delivery from bondage that began a new life of light and faith. To accept the message and to start out on the Christian way is to follow a way that rises above all other customs, which spreads outwards to all people and which will last for eternity (I.15). Baptism is not an end in itself, but simply the door to a life in Christ, the journey of following his gospel. That gospel does not destroy ordinary life and the culture around it, but brings it to a perfection which it already knows it needs. Muirchú thinks of the gospel in a manner analogous to the way Aquinas would later speak of grace: 'Grace does not tear away nature, but completes it.' If you want to envisage what is central to this mystery of Christian faith, then for Muirchú the answer lies in the celebration of the Paschal Mystery on that 'most blessed of all nights' whose power 'dispels all evil' and reconciles humanity with God. Muirchú has been the butt of many jokes for his pseudo-history, but his liturgical sense leaves little to be desired. He had an understanding of the place of the Easter Vigil – and assumed a similar understanding among his readers – such as modern liturgical scholars have desired for a century, often with little success, to restore to the average parish.

MACC CUILL'S JOURNEY

The third story I wish to highlight from Muirchú is his version of the story in Cassian of Abba Moses who went from being a murderer to being a penitent monk to being a sage of the monastic life. The story is that of the most wicked, proud and impious of men, Macc Cuill (I.23). This wicked ruler was in the habit of killing travellers through his territory, and so when he heard that Patrick was coming his way, he laid a trap to kill him. But Patrick as an apostle is preserved from the cunning of men (cf. Luke 10:19) and his miraculous deliverance brings about Macc Cuill's conversion: he declares his belief, confesses his sins and recognises that he needs penance. Patrick directs that he must abandon everything and, with just one shirt for covering, set off in a small boat upon the sea without oar or rudder – he must put himself completely at the disposition of divine Providence. So Macc Cuill is set adrift and brought by God's grace to a distant land where he is found by two holy spiritual guides, the bishops Conindrus and Rumilus. Macc Cuill becomes their disciple and 'trained his body and soul by following their rule'. Eventually, he becomes so holy that he finishes his life as a bishop!

The story is enough to make us wince. It seems to have the same subtlety as the instant conversions from one soap powder to another in a TV commercial. Likewise, the whole tale is cosy and churchey – it should come as no surprise that the Muirchú who sees being a bishop as a direct indication of holiness of life was himself an important churchman. However, such criticism aside, it does show his concern to stress that there is no one beyond the reach of conversion, mercy and a life of holiness. The characters in the tale may wholly lack depth – a feature they share with similar moral tales before and since – but the message comes across clearly: penitence can be the beginning of a new life and 'though your sins are like scarlet, they shall be as white as snow' (Isaiah 1:18).

I have chosen just three incidents from a single saint's *Vita* to convey a taste of the sort of materials that were being put forward in these 'presentations' on what constitutes the holy life. They simultaneously amused, amazed and edified, and through the repetition of the stories and the motifs they conveyed a message that within every person's life there had to be room for providence, penitence and perfection.

THE CIRCULAR JOURNEY

The other story I want to consider is the anonymous *Nauigatio sancti Brendani abbatis* (the *Voyage of St Brendan the Abbot*). Unlike Muirchú's *Vita*, this was written with a monastic audience in mind who understood the daily office, knew each psalm by its opening line, and could spot antiphons and other scriptural and liturgical cues. Moreover, it assumes that its audience knows the rudiments of exegetical method for it is self-consciously allegorical.

One of the difficulties faced by those who saw the *Nauigatio* as the narrative of some half-forgotten 'real' voyages was that the journey lacked a destination: they sail around in circles for seven years. But the real question is why they started out on such a wandering in the first place. The answer lies in the first chapter which is intended to show the whole monastic journey in a vignette, and to be a 'spiritual taster' of what must be every monk's desire. Having tasted this end – equivalent to having received a sacrament – the monks are strengthened and given the determination to pursue their true homeland although it will mean an arduous and sometimes fearful navigation. For the monk-sailors, to arrive is to begin, to grow is to move in rhythm with the seasons and the liturgy, and life's aim is to resemble the perfect liturgy of heaven.

THE THREE STEPS

The whole tale begins with a holy man Barrind arriving at St Brendan's monastery and telling him and his monks of his experience. Here is the first step – the actual monastery of Brendan and his monks is the island of Ireland, and is just one more ordinary monastery. Barrind tells of another monastery which he has visited: the island monastery of St Mernóc which is near Slieve League in Donegal; to reach it Barrind had to make a journey of three days. This is the second place, a second island, and a second stage in the monastic life, and it is called (echoing the garden in Genesis 2:8) the Island of Delights. It is quite small – it only takes a day to walk around it – but it is the perfect monastery, for on his arrival the monks all swarm out from their scattered dwellings to meet their visitor. But if they are scattered in their cells, they are united in one faith, share one table and have one liturgy. Their celebration of the office leaves nothing to be desired, their diet is one of perfect abstinence, and they even keep the Great Silence at night perfectly and without any disruption. The description of the island owes much to that of the monks of Nitria in Rufinus' translation of the *History of the Monks of Egypt* (*Historia monachorum in Aegypto*), but even more to Cassian: while Brendan's monastery represents the active life, that of Mernóc represents the contemplative life. While he is there on the second island, Barrind is told of yet another place: the Promised Land of the Saints, to which he then sets sail. However, the journey between the second and third places cannot be measured in miles or days. Having left Mernóc's island his boat was enveloped in a dense fog that veiled the third place, and when they emerge out of the fog they have left the limitations of space and time behind them. While the Island of Delights echoes Nitria, the third place is identical with the

New Jerusalem in Apocalypse 21 – 22. There is no day or night, there is neither sun nor moon, for the 'Lord Jesus Christ is the light of this island'. It has no temple for it is the very place of the eternal, heavenly liturgy; all its plants are in flower, it is full of precious stones, a river runs through its middle, and those there want for nothing. Even after fifteen days one still has not walked around it, for it is beyond measuring. This third place is the heaven towards which all humans must journey, the destination to which each must direct her or his boat of flesh, where each finds her or his true home, and it is the end anticipated in all earthly liturgy which takes place in time and is, therefore, only partial. Barrind leaves the place that he has visited and knows that it is very close to Mernóc's island, and thus he can say of that perfect monastery (as was said of the earthly Jerusalem in Genesis 28:17) that those monks 'are, without doubt, living at the very gate of Paradise'.

We should think of the Barrind tale somewhat like this:

A	B	C
[Ireland]	Island of Delights	Promised Land
Our everyday life	Mernóc's Island	of the Saints
Active life	Contemplative life	Beyond contemplation
Average temporal liturgy	Perfect temporal liturgy	Perfect eternal liturgy

The first two locations are presented as places as well as states and they share with each other the most basic structure of the finite creation: space and time, which of their nature are numbered. B is a fixed distance of earthly travel from A, and quite close to an actual place in the landscape. But while B is close to C, the distance between them cannot be numbered. C belongs not to the limited material creation characterised by temporal and spatial restrictions, but to the new creation when this world has passed away (Revelation 21:1); this is not the earthly Church but the eternal Church of the saints which dwells in the direct light of Christ, and, behold, 'his face, and his name shall be on their foreheads' (Revelation 22:4). Although C is 'close' to B, its closeness is not like that of A and B. It is veiled from A and B, and entry to it is guarded by an angel. Anyone can sail from A to B, but only those who are found worthy of the Promised Land can move from B to C.

There are other connections and disconnections. Between A and B there is the earthly, temporal liturgy: marked out by the sun and moon, the constant trickle of praise, wafting up like incense moment by moment. However, there is also difference. On B the liturgy is perfect, for the monks' discipleship is perfect, and the daily round of eating, sleeping and praying is without falter. Their harmony is expressed in the unity of faith, worship and community life. In an actual monastery, such as A, there were divisions, factions, breaches of rules of diet and discipline, and – as we still know only too well – even the best-laid plans for a regular and appropriate liturgy just kept going astray. So B shared a temporal liturgy with A, and both are distinct from the time-free (eternal) liturgy of C; but B shares a perfection, a unity of mind and heart and voice, with C. While A is a muddle which should be like B, B itself is a reflection and anticipation of C. Likewise, B shares the same space with A, yet it shares a spirit of love with C.

The lesson of the Barrind tale is simultaneously clear and veiled: Mernóc's island stands as the sacrament between this world and the Christian Promised Land. While every island stood as a microcosm to society of the Christian life, so there, on B, was the kind of life which each monastery must seek. Moreover, it is not an ideal in some higher world: it is the perfect monastery in this world and can be reached. It is the holy place that is the transformation of this world, and the taste of the world to come. The final destination cannot be reduced to a measured progress, it is beyond a mysterious veil and entry is a grace, but it too is within reach: it is close to the perfect monastery and many things there, on B, directly anticipate it. The invitation to enter into the sacramental world is that of travelling to a state of life which is at the portal of heaven. A is where we are now, C is where we desire to end up, and the stepping-stone is B. Incidentally, we see in the *Nauigatio* the transformation of the binary Augustinian image of a sacrament (a sign pointing to a reality) into something which resembles the later threefold division of the 'sign just in itself' (*sacramentum tantum*) – this is A, for every monastery points to the things of heaven just by being a monastery; then there is the 'reality itself' (*res tantum*) – this is C, the actual end that is desired by all who follow Christ; and thirdly, the 'sign-cum-reality' (*res et sacramentum*) – this is B, when the qualities of the end have been achieved in this life.

The knowledge of these two higher states/places is not something that Brendan finds out for himself, rather it is told to him by one to whom it has been revealed. Thus Barrind is the archetypal apostle, the one sent to bring the news of the life prepared for the saints and to offer guidance about how to get there. Brendan and his companions are, in turn, the perfect disciples: once they have heard of the better, heavenly, country prepared for them by God, they desire it (Hebrews 11:16), and make ready to set off to achieve it.

WE ARE SAILING . . .

The image that the *Nauigatio* presents of Brendan and his initial fourteen companions in pursuit of a more perfect holiness, the state of contemplation such as on Mernóc's island, is that of a journey sailing around the ocean. The motif of the boat implies that they are like the disciples in the boat in the Gospels (Matthew 8), and their willingness to continue on in the boat is that they shall no longer be 'men of little faith'. Entrusting themselves to the boat, although they have oars, sail and rudder, is an act of abandonment to Providence. When-

ever there are difficulties these are the very times when
Brendan tells them that they must not use the oars but wait
on what God has prepared for them. The sailing becomes a
detailed round of prayer, fasting and avoiding temptations
from the devil. They are set traps such as food when they are
hungry, comfort when tired, and riches and jewellery that
bring out their covetousness. But this is balanced by a perfect
celebration of the liturgy: the office is elaborate and is celebrated at the correct times; each feast of the year is kept
properly with its octave. This perfection is not something they
have to achieve just once, but daily; and they celebrate the
whole year not just once, but seven times. They have to learn
to master the temptations to evil and the distractions that can
pull them away from the true monastic life. The centre of the
year is the Easter Vigil, and the centre of the liturgy is
the Eucharist, and not an antiphon is missing from the Work
of God.

The sailing encounters certain places that return each year,
other places are seen only once, but in every case they are
seeing the wonders of the Lord which are at once terrifying and
attractive. For Easter each year the Lord provides a wondrous
beast, named Iasconius, upon which they celebrate; on another
occasion they meet an evil beast and see the power of God in
destroying it. They meet both good places and bad. Among the
good, they arrive on islands which are exemplary monasteries
already, such as the community of Abbot Ailbe. They also
arrive at islands which are the hermitages of anchorites, and
some of the sailors opt to take on this life themselves. On the
other hand, they see the power of the demons that are on
the edge of this world and the greater power of grace in scat-
tering them, and they even sail close to the gates of hell seeing
and smelling the telltale signs of its punishments. On the
positive side they meet the 'first' hermit, as described by
Jerome in his *Vita Pauli*, except he is now on his own island
rather than in a hot sandy desert, and recognise him as the
archetypal good monastic disciple. While by way of warning
they meet 'unhappy Judas', who also has an island of his own,

and who is the paradigm of the bad disciple who leaves and betrays his master.

After seven years of adventure and monastic discipline they are at last ready to enter the Promised Land. However, they may not enter and remain in it, for the present they are only given a visit, like Mernóc and Barrind had been. They must return to this side of the fog for now, but can bring with them some of its precious stones and some samples of its fruits. To possess the land rather than just its tasters and tokens – its sacraments – they must await 'the end of their pilgrimage' says Brendan, 'but that day draws near when you will sleep with your fathers'. Returning to where they set out from, they can now all pass through the Island of Delights – seven years of monastic devotion and trial has brought A to the same state as B, and both are close to C, indeed the veil of fog is only as far distant as the day when they will sleep with their fathers (a complex image based on Genesis 49:29), their pilgrimage over.

... HOME AGAIN

We have examined two popular texts from the Celtic world of the early Middle Ages. They are at once strange in their images and conventions, while familiar in the basic Christian questions they seek to address. We might dismiss them as a mix of silly lore or the equivalent of our science fiction, but that would ignore the fact that these authors, and many others like them, were serious religious writers who sought to render their demanding message in a form suitable to those who were, like the Corinthians, not yet capable of solid food (1 Corinthians 3:2). In all their stories they kept in mind that all of them were on a pilgrimage which would, they hoped, end in the heavenly Jerusalem – it is a motif that pops up not only in the *Nauigatio* but in exegesis, hagiography and hymnody – 'for now' they saw 'in a mirror dimly, but then face to face' (1 Corinthians 13:12).

O God, to whom all is known and who lays bear all hidden things, you know my heart's distress. So I beseech you that from your majesty you might mercifully grant to me, a sinner, a revelation of the secrets [of the creation] which I behold with my eyes. But I do not presume to ask this from my merits or station, but depending on your immense clemency.

(A prayer put into the mouth of Brendan, *Nauigatio* 11).

6. JOURNEYS OF RETURN

A CONSTANT TENSION

Deep within the Christian imagination are two notions that are radically at odds with one another. The first is that God is a stern judge who punishes transgressors for their wrong actions and breaches of his law. The second is that God is a merciful, forgiving healer who seeks out sinners not to punish, but to forgive them. While theologians and apologists have expended much energy and ink trying to show that this is a 'both . . . and . . .' rather than an 'either . . . or . . .' situation, for most Christians it has been a case that one image has been dominant and the other relegated to a siding. At some points in our life one or other may seem to make more sense: sometimes we want a merciful God for ourselves and a punitive God for others; while by contrast some people who preach a merciful God to others expect that it will be a punitive and exacting God they themselves will meet. This has been one of the great tensions of Christianity, and it defies attempts to banish it with simple slogans such as 'Old Testament = God of Judgement; New Testament = God of Love'. The tension has been there all the time, and indeed continues.

Its origins are not important for us here, but we should note that it was already present in the early Church. We hear the judgement theme in sayings such as: 'Make friends quickly with your accuser, while you are going with him to court, lest your accuser hand you over to the judge, and the judge to the guard, and you be put in prison; truly, I say to you, you will never get out till you have paid the last penny' (Matthew

5:25–26). We hear the merciful Jesus in: 'I tell you, there will be more joy in heaven over one sinner who repents than over ninety-nine righteous persons who need no repentance' (Luke 15:7). Those early Christians even saw this tension in the reactions of Jesus to his own attackers. We think of the gentle words from the cross: 'Father, forgive them; for they know not what they do' (Luke 23:34); but there is also, 'woe to that man by whom he is betrayed!' (Luke 22:22), and several traditions about the kind of death Judas met. For every text stressing mercy, one can find one stressing the Lord as the just judge; and Christians have invoked his judgement as often as his forgiveness. Therefore, it should be no surprise that there has been a continuing tension among Christians between those who have wanted to stress God's loving understanding and have seen their opponents as 'rigorists' or having missed the centrality of love, and those who have seen a betrayal of the demands of divine justice by those who 'go soft on sin' or who see in gentleness the sell-out of 'cheap grace'.

Accepting this constant tension let us note two things. First, at various times in the Church's history one or other aspect of this tension will set the tone of preaching, legislation by synods and bishops, and also pastoral structures. Second, and of great importance for this book, how Christians relate to this tension will be a basic determining factor in their spirituality. Those who emphasise the demands of the Lord will be anxious to see the Christian message as a challenge and will accept, as almost inevitable, that there will be clashes between those demands and human nature. It will affect how they perceive the body (its needs become temptations), society (it is always in danger of immoral anarchy), and the Church (losing people is simply the price of being counter-cultural). Moreover, as we look back on periods when this aspect has been dominant, in the fourth and fifth centuries or again in the modern period, we see that there arises a need to justify human failures in discipleship through a view of sin which understands it as a fundamental failure in human nature. Most famously, this was the preached notion of 'original sin' which stresses its 'effects' which are untouched by baptism: weakened will, darkened under-standing, and profound inclinations to evil. Corresponding with this there is a tendency to present the distance between the awesome holiness of God and sinful humanity. God seems distant not only as a Ruler, but in that there seems little intervention by Christ's love through the sacraments to effect change in the human condition. By contrast, those who see God as healer present him as far closer to the human situation, and the disruption of sins seems far more piecemeal: there are problems here, there and everywhere, but we are weak creatures and it is only through the constant help of Christ's grace that we are enabled to grow. There is, from this perspec-tive, far less emphasis on finding a single fundamental flaw, nor an in-built suspicion of nature around us. A maxim of discipleship becomes to take 'where one is at' as one's starting point and move one step forward. Within this view of the Christian life, the *process* of life, rather than its state of grace at a fixed moment, becomes the criterion of holiness. In setting out this contrast there is, of course, exaggeration, for real people do not divide into categories neatly. But keeping the contrast in mind helps us to understand the shift in theology and practice that occurred in the Celtic churches in the early Middle Ages and their major contribution to western Christ-ianity. However, we must remember that these extremes exist in tension: in every real situation, be it a homily, a pastoral manual or an action, there will be some blending of both per-ceptions of the Christian message.

THE PATRISTIC DEADLOCK

When Patrick arrived from Britain to preach in Ireland he brought with him the then widespread practice of the western Church which dealt with sin through 'public penance'. This had codified as God's will a number of practices which had grown in the previous centuries, particularly in the fraught times of guilt and recriminations following bouts of per-secution. By the later fourth century there was general agreement in the West that baptism was the act of rebirth for people who had suffered spiritual death through sin. They emerged to life with sin removed and clothed in the white garment of spotless innocence. But what happened after that? To the preachers the situation was clear: they were not to sin any more! But as a later Irish saying puts it, 'nature will always break out through the eye of the cat!' – sins were committed. The Church's reply came in the form of a distinction. First, the everyday trespasses were forgiven through prayer and acts of penitence, and were seen as mentioned in the Our Father: 'forgive us . . . as we forgive'. But what happened with the more serious sins that formed the second category of sins that destroyed the life of baptism? These were seen as being grouped around three crimes: murder, apostasy and fornication. Apostolic authority for this group was claimed in Acts 15:29. For these the way out was through a second, 'laborious baptism' of public penance – excommunication for years of penitence followed by formal readmission to the eucharistic community. This was severe enough, but the real crunch came in that this 'plank after shipwreck' (St Jerome) was available *only once* in a lifetime. Moreover, the actual penance was seen in terms of the punishment of a crime: one was paying for one's wilful offences and the suffering involved was a measure of the divine justice, for the alternative was to remain in death.

The system had a problem: it did not work. 'Apostasy' was no longer a problem, 'murder' was a larger problem than church discipline, but 'fornication' created difficulties without number. Given that it was so difficult to perform penance, and that it was a 'once-only' solution, to many the prudent course was to delay baptism until as late as possible, or at least until one's 'wild oats' were sown. However, anyone who raised a criticism of the practice was cried down with cries which we can still hear today: 'going soft on crime/sin', 'betraying the sacrifice of those who died rather than yield to sin', 'being untrue to the tradition and the will of God'. Indeed, the impasse was so great that a theologian as resourceful as Augustine, when faced with those who delayed baptism (as his own mother had done for him – wisely as it turned out), could not imagine changing from the idea of 'once-only' penitence. Instead, he sought to encourage infant baptism by reminding parents that a child who died without baptism would be deprived of the joy of heaven. In effect, the mess created by public penance was destroying both the pastoral life of the Church and its theology.

The impact of this system on how people viewed the Christian life is worth noting as its echoes lasted for centuries in the West – indeed some hold that its effects are still with us. First, it altered the view of baptism from being primarily entry into Christ to escaping from punishment, and from this perspective the whole of the Christian life was one of scrambling into the lifeboat of salvation rather than seeking to be the community proclaiming the new life offered by God in Christ. Second, in making such a gap between the sins which needed penance and those which did not, it failed to see that sin is a disruption within the Christian life and that by tackling smaller problems one can discover ways to deal with more basic problems in life. Its poor psychological insight imagined a sharp line dividing two camps, the sinners and the non-sinners, and led to a separation between removing sin and growing in holiness. Several wise and gentle bishops, such as St Caesarius of Arles (*c.* 470–542), recognised these problems but synod after synod simply repeated more loudly the old 'wisdom'. To innovate, they argued, would be to fail to respect the tradition and to have sinners dictating doctrine to bishops! When lung power is confused with logic, the 'apostolic tradition' is usually with those whose voices are loudest.

THE WISDOM OF CASSIAN

Cassian is the great mediator of things eastern and monastic to the West. Indeed, when people today note relationships between Celtic monks and the desert fathers they are actually observing customs brought west by Cassian but which later disappeared within various reforms of Benedictinism. Cas-

sian's whole approach to sin was different both to that of
bishops like Augustine and Patrick, and to that of preachers
like Jerome. While they viewed sin from the point of view of
the judge administering the law who on finding a crime must
justly punish, he looked on the sin as a sign of sickness which
needed an appropriate medicine.

Cassian's concern was not the three 'great' sins, but the
whole life of holiness of a monk: how could the monk overcome
the sins that hampered him from entering into a state of
contemplation and union with God? Cassian took his theory
for dealing with this disruption brought about by sins in the
monk's life from contemporary theories of medicine. Any actual
pain or symptom from which a patient suffered, argued the
physicians, arose from some more basic disruption deep within
the person, the actual pain was just the presenting problem.
The root cause was to be explained in terms of an imbalance
of the elements and humours which constituted the person;
this then could be diagnosed and remedied, and the surface
problem would disappear. If the problem is seen as an imbalance, then a measured excess in the other direction should
just do the trick! Hence we have the medical dictum that
Cassian would make famous in spiritual direction: *contraria
contrariis sanantur* (opposites heal their opposites).

As Cassian adapted the bodily medical scheme to the soul –
he saw the way the body worked as being a simpler example
of the way God had created the workings of the whole person
– he built a theology of sin which was radically different to
most of what went before it. Every particular sin, such as an
act of gluttony when a monk devoured everything he saw on
a particular day, was symptomatic of a deeper malaise. Cassian
believed that there where eight of these more basic problems
and he called them 'principle' vices, for a 'principle' is the
source from which other things flow. Individual sins could be
traced back to one or more of the main sources. So if someone
had done something wrong, the first need was to go to a suitable physician for a diagnosis – this will become the confessor
figure later called in Irish *anamchara*. The physician must

find a remedy suited to the particular sickness and prescribe it. So if the problem is avarice, then one must practise self-denial; if laziness, then vigils; or if gluttony, fasting.

Cassian also altered the context of penance. First, the image of the one who stands in the place of Christ was shifted from that of judge to physician. Second, what one was prescribed after sin shifted from fitting punishment to appropriate medicine. And, lastly and most importantly, the emphasis shifted to the future growth in the following of Christ away from making up for past crimes. However, Cassian could not have imagined how his guidance for monks would be transformed in the matter of a few decades by clergy in Wales and Ireland.

CONVERGING INFLUENCES

The medicinal theory of Cassian combined with several other factors to produce in the sixth century a new approach to sins-after-baptism in the Celtic lands. And it is this pastoral practice that constituted their most important contribution to western Christianity. We see it now only through the manuals which they produced to help in prescribing remedies, the 'penitentials', but it involved as great a change in the view of the Christian life as it did in pastoral praxis. The development took Cassian's guide for monks and extended it to the whole Church and to every sin, including fornication and murder.

One factor contributing to the development was, probably, native law in Celtic societies. It viewed crimes in terms of one party insulting another: the insult could be repaired by fines. This when transferred to a Christian notion of sin could present the wicked act as an insult to the dignity of God and, therefore, left the sinner with a debt to be settled by penance. A second factor is the development of the notion of tears as a means of washing away sins. This came from the East through Cassian – it became a highly structured element in Byzantine theology known as 'the baptism of tears' – and its basic idea built on texts like Psalm 6:6: 'I am weary with my moaning; every night I flood my bed with tears; I drench my couch with my weeping.' If one is truly sorry for the offence caused by one's sins, expressed in sorrowful tears, then God sees this sorrow and forgives. This seems obvious to us, but it marked a revolution in theology because it made the disposition of the conscience the key to divine forgiveness.

The system can be briefly described like this. Every sin was seen as an offence by a Christian against the dignity of his or her Lord. Since the emphasis is now on the nature of an interpersonal offence, rather than the wicked act seen simply as a crime against the law, the offence varied in seriousness depending on the status, knowledge and freedom of the sinner. In this, the penitentials deal with sin in a manner similar to offences in ordinary Irish law; and in the process we have the beginnings of a moral casuistry: sins must be judged on a case-by-case basis because 'situations alter cases'. Each offence, however, springs from a deeper problem within the person – one of the eight principle vices – so the problem must be diagnosed by one who is properly trained as a physician of these spiritual/moral ailments. Having diagnosed the problem and adjudged the situation, this physician can prescribe a remedy which will both help cure the underlying problem and repay the offence to the divine dignity. Thus the person can go away confident that when the prescription is fulfilled (usually from the medicine chest of Matthew 6:2–17: prayer, fasting, almsgiving) they are healed, strengthened and loosed from their sins.

To many people today it seems rather mechanical to have a book listing offences with various demands for prayer, fasting or alms which vary with whether the person is a cleric or lay person, a man or woman or child, whether the act was committed in the heat of passion or cold-bloodedly, and whether the person was instantly sorry or only later as a result of reflection. However, that is to see the system as one of penalties, and to imagine – as many do who see the purpose of religion as the maintenance of a moral code – that an awareness of the individuality of moral goodness/wickedness is to cheapen discipleship. By placing the system within a manual it was seen to take the wisdom of the fathers and distil it into a form which could be widely used – the remedies which the spiritual masters had discovered were not restricted to those lucky enough to live near them. We may dislike the idea of a manual, but the other side of that coin is that the good news of forgiveness would not have been widely available. We should think of the penitentials in terms of the handbooks that clergy still use today to get ideas for their ministry, but more accurately in terms of the manuals about symptoms and drugs that one sees on the desk of the average physician. As regards the measuring, here too we forget that for those earlier Christians number was the indicator of the divine order: exact prescriptions suited to the disorder was the aim of the process; that the medicine should be expressed in number expressed its orderliness – and it had the psychological advantage that the penitent could accomplish the task, and then turn to the future.

Today, we are becoming increasingly aware that no two Christians relate to God in the same way – we prize this as an insight into our uniqueness and individuality – but we can see the foreshadowing of this in the distinctions made in Celtic penitential practice between persons, intentions and situations. We can look back to that praxis with its awareness that 'the Lord sees the heart' (1 Samuel 16:7) as marking a new depth of understanding human motivations, and with its emphasis on deeply felt sorrow as a turn inwards from an externalist notion of crimes to a concentration on intention. In effect, what the penitentials did was to seek a balance between a known order of right and wrong actions, and the fact that two people doing the same thing may be morally poles apart.

The system that evolved in Wales and Ireland brought penitence and the pursuit of holiness back into connection. Because each sin was a symptom to be treated and an offence to be made good, it belonged to the normal pattern of Christian life. By its very nature it was repeatable, and something which one needed to repeat as one moved through the pilgrimage of life. But this very fact of being 'repeatable' ('iteratability' is the technical term) made it radically different not only in theory, but in a most obviously practical way from the venerable traditions of public penance. This made it the subject of criticism from those who still could not leave the cul-de-sac of the older system. In turn, this meant that those who wished to use this newer discipline had to situate their practice within a whole new model of divine forgiveness.

THE MODES OF MERCY

We can see this new understanding of the forgiveness of sins as not being an exceptional act of divine and ecclesial mercy, but fitting within the whole pattern of God's dealings with humanity in the very earliest penitentials we possess from the late sixth century. However, the earliest example where the new understanding is formally laid out comes from the prologue to the *Penitential of Cummean* which dates from the seventh century. We cannot be certain why Cummean prefaced his manual with this long theoretical framework, but the most likely explanation is that it was intended to defend the insular practice of penance from those who boldly cried that it broke with the Church's tradition. This would explain Cummean's desire to locate his method within the tradition – constantly citing Scripture to show that he was not an innovator – and to suggest that his practice would be approved by the holy fathers. We might think this disingenuous, but he was not the first (that honour probably belongs to St Vincent of Lérins who died around 450) and he would not be the last who justified theological common sense through a mask of antiquity.

The title of the prologue gives us the key to his whole approach: it is about 'the medicine for healing souls'. That metaphor continues in the opening sentence: it is about 'the teachings of the earlier fathers on the remedies for wounds . . . and the medicines prescribed in Scripture'. But all these healing acts of God, along with the appropriate human therapies, have to be seen as linked within a whole hierarchy of divine, ecclesial and individual activity.

The 'first sending away of sin is through baptism with water'. Cummean's supporting text (John 3:5: 'unless one is born of water and the Holy Spirit, he cannot enter the kingdom of God') is a most interesting choice, for it stresses a view of baptism as the key to new life and the kingdom, rather than the ending of an old life and the removal of sin. The 'second is through an attitude (*affectus*) of love' and he cites Jesus' words rebuking the disciples who belittled the woman who anointed him: 'her sins . . . are forgiven, for she loved much' (Luke 7:47). The third is surprising as it places the actual giving of physical aid to the poor so high in the scheme of the Christian life: 'the third sending away is the fruit of giving alms' and he cites Sirach 3:30: 'just as water puts out a blazing fire, so giving alms extinguishes sin'. (Some people today would no longer consider Sirach to be Scripture, and put it in an inferior category labelled 'apocrypha'. However, that is a position that was formally repudiated from Augustine onwards – including writers in the Celtic lands – when the whole of the large Old Testament canon was considered to be inspired.)

The fourth 'sending away' brings in the notion of contrition. It consisted in 'a profusion of tears' and Cummean cites a garbled form of 1 Kings 21:27–29. Following upon that comes the fifth remission which is 'the declaration of crimes' (*criminum confessio*), supported by Psalm 32:5. This, in effect, neatly placed both public penance and Cummean's own practice within a larger context, and presented them as less significant for spiritual health than love, alms and internal sorrow for one's sins. The sixth is 'affliction of heart and body' – ascetical practices – based on 1 Corinthians 5:5; while the seventh is 'the amendment of life' treated as the equivalent to 'the renunciation of vices'. This is supported by John 5:14 where the act of forgiveness is linked to the notion of being made healthy and whole by Christ. This imagery of healing also appears in the eighth manner in which sins are sent away through the intercession of the saints; it cites the classic text for the practice of praying for the sick that they might be healed (James 5:14–16).

The ninth, tenth and eleventh modes of forgiveness can be seen as loosely linked by the theme that those who forgive will merit forgiveness, for 'the merciful shall obtain mercy' (Matthew 5:7), those who save others will not themselves be lost (based on James 5:20), and those who 'forgive will be forgiven' (Luke 6:37). The final mode of forgiveness is through the passion of martyrdom. The text used to support this is that of the suffering Lord forgiving the repentant thief in Luke's passion account: 'Truly, I say to you, today you will be with me in Paradise' (23:43). This twelve-fold scheme for understanding forgiveness was not original to Cummean nor to those insular church leaders who developed the system – its roots can be traced back to Cassian's *Conference* 20 – but it was a revolution in practice. What Cassian had formulated as part of a monastic way of perfection was now being treated as a general pattern for all Christians. It is hard for us to grasp how profoundly new the system was, especially when it wholly ignored the patristic arguments about penance being a once-in-a-lifetime rescue and substituted the notion of ongoing remission and improvement. A possible modern comparison would be the Roman Catholic Church ordaining women, but even that change would not have had to transcend nearly so much 'tradition'.

LIFE AS PENITENCE

The West had famously translated the opening challenge of Jesus, 'Be converted and believe in the good news' (Mark 1:15) as 'Do penance and believe . . .'. This had not been seen as located at the heart of the ongoing living of the Christian life, but as an act followed by another act of believing, after which one lived as a Christian. Now a life of penitence was seen as a norm: it was an integral part of living as a Christian that one must be rooting out sinfulness and growing in holiness. Many people see this as the basis of a continual sense of guilt, and there is probably more than a grain of truth in this, but it also brings every Christian face to face with the unpleasant reality that we must tackle our sinfulness and our basic sinful attitudes (what Cassian called our 'principle' vices) each day. We grow away from sin and towards Christ taking it one day at time; as the Irish exegetes pointed out, this was taking up the cross *daily*: 'If any man would come after me, let him deny himself and take up his cross daily and follow me' (Luke 9:23).

BY THEIR FRUITS...

No development in spirituality, and certainly none that involves a change in church praxis, produces only good fruit – somehow, someone, at some time will turn it on its head and it will become as much a distraction from discipleship as it was originally an aid to the pilgrimage of life. So it was with the practice of penitence which developed in the Celtic lands, and which – despite opposition from the odd bishop here or synod there – soon spread throughout the western Church. Thus the great benefit of making penance repeatable would come in time to be seen as the playing down of conversion, replacing it with the rattling-off of a laundry list of sins for auricular confession to a priest. What Roman Catholics call the sacrament of penance/reconciliation was a direct development from the insular practice. Equally, the notion of a measured medicinal penance suffered from inflation because amounts were expanded beyond reason when later the old fears of 'letting people off lightly' reappeared, along with the attitude that a 'light penance does not show sufficient disapproval', so that the system became unworkable. One could not argue with such hard-liners for it merely allowed them to say that common sense was 'conforming to this world' (Romans 12:2) and the very fact that everyone found it so difficult was the proof they were right, for 'Christ is the sign of contradiction' (cf. Luke 2:34). This is then seen as a self-justifying argument, rather than the fallacy of arguing in a circle. The result was a 'work around' whereby the impossible amounts of penance were 'exchanged' for more manageable amounts of prayers, alms or good works. The beginnings of the process can already be found in Ireland in the eighth century, but it reached its classic form as 'indulgences' – the very word conjures up for many the weakness of later penitential practice. However, it is not fair to those who courageously faced the pastoral impasse of the fifth century to blame them for later abuses of their creation. It is more just, and profitable, to see them as answering the most basic demands of the gospel from their resources at the time, and thus making the Christian message alive and active in their culture.

As I see it there are several important insights in the insular understanding of penance which are still important for Christians more than a millennium later:

- Humans are neither 'sinners' – in a perpetual 'state of sin' – nor 'saints' who sometimes break the law. Rather we are involved in a complex process by which we must see sinful acts as symptoms of deeper problems. The process of growing in holiness and tackling these weaknesses is one we must set out upon daily.

- In our image of human life it is important that we recognise that we are moving forward in time, and that a better future is part of the dynamic of discipleship.

- Sin is a disruption in a relationship; the most positive way to address such disruption is by analogy with sickness rather than law. Thus God is acknowledged as creator and healer in contrast to ruler and law-giver.

- The healing process for overcoming our sinful attitudes involves intersecting action by the individual, the community, which is part of Christ and which diagnoses and prescribes, and God who is the source of healing and new life. The notion that one is passive in the process, or that it can bypass the Church, or that it does not need help from beyond us, would reduce the process to simply a more elaborate form of 'new-year resolution'.

- Ritual actions related to overcoming sinfulness are less significant than living an attitude of loving, concern for the poor, and having a personal awareness of sorrow.

- Each person's pilgrimage is different – the positive side of the need for a casuistry – and one's spiritual health must be an ongoing concern in a similar way to our concern for bodily health.
- And lastly, when church people are faced with pastoral impossibilities which seem to bury them with 'tradition', rather than restating 'what has always been done', they should completely refocus their questions in terms of the more basic demands of discipleship – and see if what was an impasse turns out to be just a rumble strip on the road.

7. WALKING FORWARDS

ORDINARY LIFE

It is relatively easy to reconstruct the spiritualities of professional religious people, especially in the case of the Middle Ages that of monks, for they formally spent time considering questions about their relationship with God, they wrote about these matters in letters and books, and they lived in communities where such books were likely to survive. However, it is much more difficult to get a glimpse into what ordinary people, women and men who worked on the land or at a trade or who looked after children, believed, and how they saw the Christian life. Yet these people make up the vast majority of the communion of saints, and without their faith and work the monasteries would simply have died. Someone calculated some time ago that around AD 800 to keep one cleric engaged in full-time prayer and study there had to be fifty people engaged in agriculture. While books may be written about the spirituality of those monks, we know very little about the families who lived only hundreds of metres from the cloister but who were essential to its life. Sadly, when these Christians are mentioned today it is as if they were pathetic figures full of superstitions and silly customs about wells and relics: gullible and comic.

One way around this lack of information is to look at some of the homilies which the ordinary people would have heard. Of course, there is always a gap between what is preached and how people make sense of that message in their lives, but it does bring us closer to the faith of the majority. Several major collections of homilies have survived from the Celtic lands, many of a very catechetical kind, as well as numerous isolated sermons in Latin and the vernaculars. However, rather than 'pick and mix' I want to look at one of the smaller collections – small enough that you can read its seven model homilies in this chapter – as this gives a certain integrity.

THE COLLECTION

It is a collection of seven Hiberno-Latin sermons found in two manuscripts where each of the sermons opens with the characteristic early Irish Christian expression, 'In the name of God the Most High' (*In nomine Dei summi*). The collection is in Latin as they were intended as model sermons: the preacher could pick one ready made for use on a Sunday morning, or use it as a quarry for ideas and stories. They are simple in language and rather colourful in their vivid descriptions, but they are far from being theologically naive. We know that the collection was used widely in Celtic Christian circles before the ninth century; we see bits of these sermons in other places, for example in Anglo-Saxon sources, so they were obviously valued, and their wide use gives us added assurance that they form a window not just to one congregation but to more widely held Christian attitudes.

DATE AND ORIGINS

We cannot be precise about the age of the sermons, for the study of Celtic homiletics is still in its infancy, but we know they were certainly in use with Anglo-Saxon clergy in the Upper Rheinland in the early ninth century. Establishing the date of composition is more difficult, but the fact that two of the homilies (3 and 7) are explicitly based on the Nicene Creed does help a little, and gives us a definite pointer to the origins of the collection. These homilies are explanations by paraphrase (especially Sermon 3) and expansion (especially Sermon 7) of phrases from the creed, and presuppose that this text was already well known by the target audience. Since such familiarity was through its use in the eucharistic liturgy, then the beginning of that usage supplies us with a date for the collection. The creed was introduced into the eucharistic liturgy in Spain in the late sixth century where it was located just before the Lord's Prayer. It spread next to Ireland. There the creed moved to the now familiar place in the Liturgy of the Word after the Gospel, as can be seen from the Stowe Missal (written sometime between 790 and 820). Then it spread to Anglo-Saxon England, and from there, through Alcuin, to the Continent where it is found in the palace chapel of Charlemagne at Aachen in the early 790s. It appears that it spread slowly on the Continent, despite approval for its use from Pope Leo III in 810, mainly in centres with insular links, for it is mentioned in only a few ninth-century Carolingian liturgical sources. This pattern for the use of the creed exactly fits our homilies: they were in use in Anglo-Saxon circles on the Continent in the early ninth century, and come from a liturgical environment with a firm familiarity with the creed, such as Ireland. Unfortunately, since the Stowe Missal is our earliest fixed date, we cannot determine when the use of the creed began in Ireland, but we could presume that it was in use by, at least, the early eighth century. So we can suggest that these homilies originated in Ireland in the eighth century at the latest; yet they could be older, for the criterion of their age is that they must be subsequent to the introduction of the creed there.

Let us turn now to the homilies themselves. As with most sermons from the period they drip with quotations from Scripture – some taken in context, some out of context – and to recall those echoes for us, I have inserted the sources of the quotations in square brackets [ ].

SERMON 1

In the name of God most high [cf. Hebrews 1:7].

It is indeed fitting that we should first hear justice and then understand it [cf. Proverbs 2:2 and 9]. Then we ought to offer the fruit of those teachings we have understood, just as the apostle tells us: 'it is not the hearers, but the doers of the law who will be justified' [Romans 2:13]. Thus in whatever manner we have tasted life, we do not rest from fulfilling the law [cf. Matthew 5:17], since the taste of death [cf. John 8:52] is that which awaits us in the future. So the prophet foretold: 'who is the man who can live and not' taste 'death' [Psalm 89:48]? But in whatever way death was given 'in Adam' [1 Corinthians 15:22; cf. Romans 5:12], so it rules in all his sons and at life's end this is what the future holds for each and every human being. Then two opponents will come to meet him: [one] an enemy, an Ethiopian black as a raven [cf. Song of Solomon 5:11] or quenched coals, the other an army in garments white as snow [Revelation 7:9]. And over the soul of each one they will hold a contest to see if he be just or unjust; and both protagonists shall know to which of them he belongs.

If in this contest the demons find that the person is one of their allies they all rejoice, and by the same token the angels are saddened.

The demons say: 'That man is ours! He was unarmed in the battle, he was not brave, and he failed to bear the arms of Paul the apostle, "the shield of faith" "and the sword of the" holy "Spirit which is the word of God" and the "breastplate of justice" and "the helmet of salvation" [Ephesians 6:14–17] which he ought to have carried for warfare against us. Arouse him [cf. Matthew 10:8] and drag him from his body and give him terrors and horrors and lead him to the terrible places where he will see all the trials.'

Then that soul, who sees nothing in the present life, says: 'O great distress!' Having heard it all before, the demons reply: 'Even greater is about to be given to you. We have tethered you to the first-formed Satan who is bound with his attendant mob in the deepest hole' [cf. Revelation 20:1–2].

Then the soul says: 'Great is the darkness!' The demons reply: 'It will get even worse for you.'

Then a third time it says: 'The way is rough!' The demons

reply: 'The future is even rougher for you. You will see the bitterness of your kind who have abandoned "the tents of the just" [Psalm 117:15].'

Then the demons will say: 'Divide up into two opposing groups, one group to start and the other to follow and sing to him songs from the songs of David: "Why do you rejoice in evil-doing?" [Psalm 51:3]; and then again "God has plucked you out and up-rooted you from the land of the living" [Psalm 51:7]; and then say: "There is no help for him in his God" [Psalm 3:3].'

Michael meanwhile never abandons a soul until he allots it its reward before the judgement seat of the Trinity. He sees all the works that the soul has done and, holding his book [Revelation 20:12] in his hands, he lays out for it either good things or bad [Matthew 12:35]. And if the angels find the soul to belong to them, they rejoice while the demons grieve. Then the angels say: 'That man is ours for he was strong [1 Peter 5:9] in the conflict and solid in the battle and was welcoming [Matthew 25:35] and merciful [James 5:11]. He was helpful, remembered nothing evil, guarded every good, and he did not push away the arms of Paul the apostle, namely, "the shield of faith" "and the sword of the" Holy "Spirit which is the word of God" and "the breastplate of justice" and "the helmet of salvation" [Ephesians 6:14–17] which are the instruments of our war. Arouse him [Matthew 10:8] gently from his body so that he sees nor feels nothing of fear or sadness or doubt.'

Then the soul says: 'Great is the light!'

The angels responding say: 'It will be greater for you yet and you will see the brightness of God as it were "face to face" and not as "in a mirror" [1 Corinthians 13:12] nor through a veil in the way that the sons of Israel looked on the face of Moses' [Exodus 34:33–35].

The soul then speaks again: 'Great is the joy!'

The angels reply: 'It will be even greater for you. You will see the joy of the angels coming to meet you with their divine singing, and with all the saints saying "These are they who have come through the great tribulation and have washed

their garments and made them white in the blood of the Lamb"
[Revelation 7:14].'

And the soul spoke a third time: 'The road is sweet!'

The angels replied: 'It is going to be even sweeter for you.
We are going to lead you to the tents of the just [Proverbs
14:11] away from the haunts of the wicked.'

Then the angels said: 'Divide up into two armies, one group
to start and the other to follow and sing to him songs from the
songs of David where he manifests the blessedness of the soul
on entering into the house of God' [stock phrase, e.g. Matthew
12:4]. They said: 'Blessed is he whom you choose and take up,
O Lord; he will dwell in your tents. We will be filled with good
things in your house. Holy is your temple and wonderful in
equity' [Psalm 64:5]. 'There is no acceptance of persons there,'
[Romans 2:11] nor nobility of kind, for God 'rewards each one
according to his works' [Romans 2:6 and Matthew 16:27]. The
wicked depart 'into eternal fire' [Matthew 25:41], 'but the just
into eternal life' [Matthew 25:46].

Some notes

The basic imagery is that of the final judgement scene at the
coming of the Son of Man in glory in Matthew 25:31–46. It
takes the basic message of the scene, and many of the characters such as angels and demons, and turns it all into a colourful
piece of story-telling. The notion of judgement is presented in
a two-handed way: 'on the one hand' and 'on the other'. These
are seen as perfect contrasts (the depths and pains of hell
compared with the heights and joy of heaven) and each is the
fruit of a way of life. Thus this is a variant on the theme that
there are two ways, two paths, two roads which a person might
take in the journey of life – this is a theme which goes back
to the very earliest strands of Christian preaching as seen in
the *Didache* (mid to later first century). The sermon also brings
out two other points with care. First, while heaven and hell,
the saved and the damned, may be compared and contrasted,
one cannot compare God and Satan: one is creator, the other

is made; nor the power of God which knows no limits with that of Satan and his angels who are only powerful in that the humans follows them. Second, life is seen as a contest where the Christian must take up the appropriate armour and weapons, and then 'fight the good fight' (1 Timothy 6:12). While we may find its imagery too colourful, its presentation of the task facing Christians shows that the prize of faith is within their reach, and that the good Christian life is one that they can live through the pursuit of justice.

SERMON 2

In the name of God most high.

Come together frequently to the church! Declare your sins to the priests; and on account of your sins ask them to ask God that he be generous to you.

You ought to offer offerings every Day of the Lord for your-selves and for your families. For what is worthy and acceptable to God is this, that Christians (who often act negligently) should wash away their sins through holy offerings, through alms, through pure prayer and contrition of heart, and through fasting and abstinence. And in this way you ought to act in all things.

Consider yourselves! For what were you born into the world? For what other than that you should do good? And if you do something through ignorance or stupid contrariness, it is necessary that you amend for this through a good work, and seek that it will be brought home to your memory that the way you live with your wife will be in the manner that is fitting for a Christian.

Lay out honour to your parents [Exodus 20:12]!

You should love your wife [cf. Ephesians 5:25]!

You should teach your children the law of God and the catholic [law] with the greatest discipline so that they may know how to love and fear God, and to honour their parents – for this is what is pleasing to God [cf. Psalm 67:17 and 1 Corinthians 10:5].

Above all you must abstain from foul talk. Do not detract from your neighbour, and if he does something that displeases you, talk with him and admonish him with charity; and if that profits you, you will save yourself also.

Take care about drunkenness on all occasions, for it is a great destroyer of the soul. Just as fire easily sets fire to the stubble and the light straw, so drunkenness corrupts the soul and casts it into great sin.

When you enter the house of God, reflect with great fear that then you are going to your master so that you can beseech him for what you have neglected, and you are asking for a life which perhaps you do not deserve on account of your sins. And while you are standing in the church, always have your mind raised to God, and always watch with the eyes of your heart how consolation is offered to you by God from on high. If you do this often, and you have God always before your eyes, then the Adversary [cf. 1 Peter 5:8] will flee from you and will not prevail against you. Then the angel of the Lord is a helper with you in these good things, where he looks through your mind to see if you have a prepared soul. Reflect that 'God is honourable' [Sirach 2:13] and that he accepts the prayers of those who pray with purity, and he does not delay his promises. At once he received the cries and lightens and stretches out his help to those who are sorry.

How is it possible to perform something good which you have in your minds? If the last day finds you with these good works, then the angels will greet you and will receive you with joy, and they will lead you before the tribunal of judgement, there you will receive according as you have done. This should not be put to one side among you, for our Lord Jesus Christ has announced this to us, through the holy scripture which is read each day in the catholic church, that the end of this world is coming closer every day, and the signs which predict it are being found each day [cf. Luke 21:11]. I hope his coming will be in the very near future and that he will judge the whole universe with fire [cf. 2 Peter 3:7–12]. Whatever is made plain to our eyesight, we know this: that 'on the last day' when the

sin of humans will be complete, the Lord will not wish to
endure this any more, then fire will come forth from the Lord
to burn the whole universe with all the things that are in it,
and everything will be reduced to nothing on account of the
sins of human beings. Then next, and after not many days,
almighty God will rebuild all the better things that had been
in it, and it will be the resurrection of human beings, and all
human beings, both good and bad, shall have to rise in one
moment. And then our Lord Jesus Christ has to come to judge
where he has placed them, 'and all the angels with him'
[Matthew 25:31] and all 'the powers of the heavens will be
shaken' [Matthew 24:29]. 'Then' the king, the redeemer of all,
'will sit' in the seat 'of his majesty and before him will be
gathered all the nations, and he will separate them one from
another as a shepherd separates the sheep from the goats'
[Matthew 25:31–32]. 'He will place those' who are good to his
right, but the evil ones to his left [cf. Matthew 25:33].

'Then' he 'will say to those on his right, "Come, O blessed of
my Father, receive the kingdom which is prepared for you from
the beginning of the world." ' And he will continue saying: 'For
I was hungry and you gave me to eat, I was thirsty and you
gave me to drink, I was naked and you covered me, sick and
in prison and you visited me.' Then the just will answer him,
'O Lord, when did we see you hungry, or thirsty, or naked, or
sick or in prison, and serve you?' Then he will say to them, 'As
much as you did it to one of the least of these, you did it to
me' [Matthew 25:34–40].

And then he will say to those who are on his left, 'Depart
from me, you cursed, into the eternal fire which is predestined
for the devil and his angels. I hungered and you did not give
me to eat, I thirsted and you did not give me to drink, I was
a stranger and you did not welcome me, I was naked and you
did not cover me, sick and in prison and you did not minister
to me' [Matthew 25:41–44].

Consider, my children, the great piety of God [cf. Sirach
2:13], and ask that in the coming judgement that he will not
reprove our sins, nor say 'You have done evil', but rather that

he chide those who have acted and have not mended their ways. So this is something to be considered by us in all things while each of us is able, while each has time and has his reward in his hands. In so far as he has the upper hand, each person can buy himself back so that when it comes to him he will not be with the evil ones sent into hell, but with those who on account of good works are received into the heavenly kingdom. For there will be a separation between the good and the bad, after which none of the good will be with the bad, nor any of the bad with the good: each will have that sort of companion he joined with in this life and has willed to be with forever, goodness has not ebbed from the good person, nor evil from the sinners and the negligent who have walked with proud hearts [cf. Proverbs 21:4] and in the desires of the flesh [cf. Galatians 5:16–17] who, having finished this life, shall live forever in the eternal tortures without either end or remedy.

Just as the Lord has offered and promised that those who love and fear him, and keep his commandments, shall rejoice with him without end in the heavenly kingdom, so those who consent to the allure of the Adversary [cf. 1 Peter 5:8] and have not improved their ways will be tortured without end.

So the Almighty saves us and rescues us with the greatest love. And he gives this to us so that when we do evil, we can improve; and so with that help be found worthy to come to the everlasting good life, he helping us who lives and reigns forever and ever. Amen.

Some notes

This sermon too dwells on the future judgement with its long reflection on how that event should cause its hearers to live their lives. However, before the reflection on judgement it lays out its basic code for ordinary people about how they ought to live their lives. Significantly, the author assumes that his hearers are married men, and he only mentions women (as wives) incidentally. The moral code is a simple one: prayer, fasting, alms – the key elements in early preaching on general

Christian discipline. Then come some rules about family life and some of the faults that seem to attract preachers perennially: drink and bad language.

This emphasis on the final judgement has been balanced, in contrast to later apocalypticism, by two other elements. First, the major demands of Christ's law are not presented in terms of an individualistic morality, but in terms of a social concern for those in need whom one encounters. It maintains the sacramentalism of the Gospels: one loves Christ by loving the least person who is in need. Second, the sermon assumes that in the growth in the Christian life there will be a frequent need for forgiveness, and that this will be forthcoming from a forgiving God. That was the sermon's opening point which is repeated in the conclusion: it is God's love which draws humans to a better life.

SERMON 3

In the name of God most high.

In the first place, it is proclaimed through the pages of sacred scripture, that all the inhabitants, both believers and unbelievers alike, scattered over the whole earth believe faithfully in the almighty trinity: the Father, the Son, and the Holy Spirit, three Persons, one God, remaining in one divine substance; who is the creator of the universe, i.e. *the heavens and the earth* and the sea, *maker of all things visible and invisible*, and the creator of the angels and archangels and of the whole celestial army of powers.

We are instructed by divine oracles that this God of great power is above all, and that we should love our creator 'from our whole heart and from out whole soul and with all our strength' [Mark 12:30].

Similarly, for all those who desire to reach eternal life, it is most necessary to believe and confess Jesus Christ our Lord. That he is truly the only-begotten Son of the Father, who *for our salvation came down from the heavens* sent by the Father, *and was conceived by the Holy Spirit* in the womb of Saint

Mary ever virgin. And that he was born 'in Bethlehem of Judah' [Matthew 2:5], the first-born [Matthew 1:25] of his mother according to the predictions of the holy prophets.

In his divinity he is, before the ages, the source of the universes, without any beginning he remains with the Father, being *the Word through whom all things were made* [John 1:3]. As a human being he humbly and mercifully assumed flesh, *was crucified under Pontius Pilate*, and died, and *was buried, and on the third day he rose* from the dead in the same flesh, and in the same body after forty days [cf. Acts 1:3] 'he *ascended* over all the heavens' [Ephesians 4:10] and *he sits at the right hand of God*. From whence in the final time of the ages *he will come again in his glory* and of the Father and of the holy angels, the moment of the burning of the heavens and the earth [cf. 2 Peter 3:7–12], and coming with the earth trembling 'in the voice of the archangel and with the sound of the trumpet of God' [1 Thessalonians 4:16] *to judge the living and the dead* and 'to render to each one according to his works' [Matthew 16:27 and Romans 2:6]. Then there will be the everlasting *life after death* prepared for all the saints, but for the impious and the sinners there will be the eternal punishments and these will be undimmed forever.

So the Christian stands upon the foundation of faith, while he raises the structure of good works; but first those evil works which scripture prohibits are to be avoided, then the good works, which are pleasing to God [cf. 1 John 3:22], are to be built. Blessedness is prepared for those, who according to the psalmist 'move away from evil and do good' [Psalm 36:27] by the most excellent Jesus Christ, our Lord, 'to whom is glory forever and ever. Amen' [Galatians 1:5].

Some notes

This is a simple exposition of the Nicene Creed in a manner very similar to the way that exegetes worked their way through gospel passages. We are so used to 'the creed' that we do not appreciate that these were among the first Christians who met it as a text, and not as part of the baptismal rite and the liturgy of the dying in the form of questions. The notion that it was somehow a summary of Christian belief only took off with the spread of its use at the Eucharist – a practice which was spreading at the time this sermon was written. The notion that the creed is a statement of 'core' beliefs – a sort of fundamental catechism – around which 'more peripheral' beliefs cluster, is a view that would not appear until many centuries after this sermon was written.

SERMON 4

In the name of God most high.

'Seek first the kingdom of God and his justice, and all these things will be given to you' [Matthew 6:33]. We seek with the heart, we ask with the mouth, we knock with good works [cf. Matthew 7:7]. If, therefore, we relinquish all vices and all that is contrary to the will of God, we shall possess the kingdom with the angels and the archangels and the prophets, and with the apostles and martyrs, where there will be rejoicing without end, serenity with a cloud, a kingdom without turmoil.

However, not all those who seek the kingdom of this world find it; and he who has found it does not possess it forever. Everyone who seeks the kingdom of God with faith and justice finds it [cf. Matthew 7:8], and he who has found it is never sent away. But the kingdom of this world is like a shadow on water, and 'the glory' of man is like 'the flower of the grass'. But 'the grass withers and its flowers fall away' [1 Peter 1:24]. But the kingdom of this world is like a dream in the night; but the friends of God remain forever [cf. Psalm 116:2]. For all 'those things which are seen are temporal, but those things which are not seen are eternal' [2 Corinthians 4:18]. Therefore, 'Seek first the kingdom of God and his justice, and all these things will be given to you' [Matthew 6:33].

So one should first seek the kingdom through good works, that is charity and fasting and prayer and humility and benevolence; and whatever we need, that will be placed before us, and he gives us immortality and eternal life for our good works. God does not seek the start of the work but its end.

Some notes

As a short exhortation to keep moving along the journey of the Christian life, this sermon is hard to better. Note first its confidence in the justice of God, Christians live in a cosmos: 'Everyone who seeks the kingdom of God with faith and justice finds it, and he who has found it is never sent away.' And second, its sacramental view of that cosmos: 'But the kingdom of this world is like a shadow on water...' The journey's destiny lies beyond the visible end of the path.

SERMON 5

In the name of God most high.

'Fear the Lord' and 'love' always [Psalm 33:10 and 30:24], for the Lord is gentle and generous with those who love him; but he is furious and angry with sinners and with those who have contempt for his commandments.

> God teaches vigils,
> The devil teaches sleepiness.

> God teaches fasting,
> The devil teaches saturation.

> God teaches generosity,
> The devil teaches avarice.

> God teaches chastity,
> The devil teaches fornication.

> God teaches gentleness,
> The devil teaches anger.

> God teaches patience,
> The devil teaches impatience.

God teaches humility,
The devil teaches pride.

God teaches peace,
The devil teaches controversy.

God teaches love of neighbour,
The devil teaches killing.

If we consent to the Lord, he leads us into the kingdom.

If we consent to the devil, he leads us into hell; hence we resist him with strength, and he flees from us.

Love the Lord for it is good, he always was, and is, and will be.

We shall reign with him without end, if 'we keep his commandments' [1 John 5:2] and we will be 'sons of God' [1 John 3:22].

Scripture speaks to each and every one of us: do not sell your wheat for straw, nor give away your light for the darkness, nor your God for a human being. The love of a human being leads to sorrow; the love of Christ enlightens the heart and leads to eternal life. So love your God as he has loved you. 'He who perseveres' [Matthew 10:22] in the love of Christ 'up to the end, he will be saved' [Matthew 24:13].

Some notes

The 'two Ways' are presented here as a collection of opposites which integrate the notion of a set of rules with that of loving one's neighbour. We may find this repetitive, but we have to imagine this being used with an almost wholly illiterate congregation where these little two-stroke statements are like nuggets for the memory.

SERMON 6

In the name of God most high.

It is fitting for each and every one of us to love his soul, just as he loves his body.

The body when it is hungry seeks food; when thirsty it seeks drink; when it is naked, clothing; when it labours it seeks rest; when it is sleepy, it seeks sleep. Just so the soul also needs these things: the food of the soul is the Word of God; its drink is prayer or wisdom; its clothes are a firm faith in Christ; its rest is truth; its sleep is humility. On this last point scripture says: 'I will overlook any other except for the one who is humble and quiet and trembles at my word' [Isaiah 66:2]; and in another place: 'he who exalts himself will be humbled, but he who humbles himself will be exalted' [Matthew 23:12]; and Christ says, 'Learn from me for I am meek and humble of heart' [Matthew 11:29]; and in another place: 'God opposes the proud, but gives grace to the humble' [James 4:6 and 1 Peter 5:5].

> So it behoves us to lift up our souls
> from the present things to the things that are absent,
> from sadnesses to joy,
> from fallen things to eternal things,
> from earthly things to heavenly things,
> from the lowest things to the high things,
> from the absence to God to his presence,
> from journeying to our own inheritance,
> from the region of death to the region of life
> in which we shall see the heavenly things 'face to face' [1 Corinthians 13:12] and the king of kings reigning over the eternal things, with whom we, destined to last, will reign always without end in the eternal kingdoms of the eternal king. Amen.

Some notes

In using the body as its basic reference point this sermon sees it as the sacrament for the life of the Christian with God. In turn, the life of the Christian in the world must reach beyond the images and desire to encounter the Lord 'face to face'. Of the seven sermons, this is the only one which could be used without explanatory comment by believers today.

SERMON 7

In the name of God most high.

There are seven Signs which have cleansed this world.

The first Sign: the birth of our Lord Jesus Christ *from the virgin Mary*, so that we might be reborn in the innocence and simplicity of children.

The second Sign: Christ *died for us*, so that we might die to our sins.

The third Sign: *he was buried*, so that, as the apostle says, 'we might be buried with' Christ [Romans 6:4].

The fourth Sign: *he rose from the dead*, so that we might rise from the dead and from our sins to the perfect life and into spiritual bodies.

The fifth Sign: *he ascended into heaven*, that we might follow in his footsteps through our power, that is through good thoughts and good words and good works.

The sixth Sign: *he sits at the right hand of God the Father*, which points to our eternal stability in the kingdom of the eternal God.

The seventh Sign: that we look forward to Christ when he will give the rewards to his saints 'on the day of judgement' according to their merits, as the apostle says: 'he who sows sparingly will also reap sparingly, and he who sows' in blessing 'will reap' in blessing in life eternal [2 Corinthians 9:6].

Some notes

This sermon recalls 'signs' in the Johannine sense of events which manifest God's glory and lead disciples to believe in Christ (cf. John 2:11). At an obvious level it is another simple exposition of the creed; however, its central message is that Christ's life is sacramental for it sets out the pattern for our own existence.

IMAGINE ...

These sermons present us with a curious mixture of warnings about judgement, exhortations to good works, and catechesis. However, when we look on them as a collection we see a particular vision of the Christian life coming into focus. It is one which finds echoes of the divine order in the human body and external world, and it sees a pattern for life in the earthly life of Jesus. Here the sacramentalism found in learned monastic texts has been brought into the common currency of preaching to women, men and children on a Sunday.

Today we would recoil from some of the imagery, and have become coy about allegorical stories such as the 'tug-o-war' between the angels and the demons for the soul; but the theology of judgement is a balanced one, and one's place at the judgement is firmly anchored in care and love of neighbour. Sacramentalism in the movement of the mind to God demands a firm commitment to social justice, for as our preacher realised: 'If someone says, "I love God", while hating his brother, he lies; for he who does not love his brother whom he sees, cannot love God whom he has not seen' (1 John 4:20). Equally, while stressing the End, the preacher also sees life as having movement at its heart: we are moving forward in every action, good and bad, but toward which destination? To read these sermons is to listen to a message from a distant place – we can barely imagine how they contributed to the spirituality of their first audience. Yet for Christians today, while these approaches are foreign, there is still a strange familiarity. There are the same scriptural and credal texts, the same challenges and fundamental beliefs, and the yet more tantalising thought: for those of us who beleive in the communion of saints the people who first heard these sermons are still our brothers and sisters 'who have preceded us' to our destination 'signed with the sign of faith'.

8. WALKING IN TIME

THE CRISIS OF TIME

In his account of being a hostage in Beirut, Brian Keenan described his tiny dismal cell and said that time meant nothing in there (*An Evil Cradling*, London 1992, p. 62). It is an extreme statement, for that was an extreme situation. Time, the very mark of constancy as it moves onwards carrying promise or foreboding tucked up in its ticking, could not be felt in that cell – was it that windowless walls and sheet-steel could exclude it? Few who read this book will have had anything like that experience, but many will have experienced the crisis of time in another way: time as the enemy who holds us in its grip. Rather than we marking our lives with time, it seems to dictate our actions second by second. Both sensations link time with being a prisoner, and that linkage is part of what separates us from the past and its perspectives on the sequences of change.

Time is all around us. Living, growth and movement suppose time as a basic element of our existence – we cannot even imagine life without it. We may say 'God is eternal' but all we mean is that if time limits us, and God is the being without limits, then the limitations that time imposes upon us do not restrict God. But what would it be like to be without time? A genuine understanding of such life is beyond us. Time impinges on our consciousness far more profoundly than simply as a reflection on our limitations as finite beings. From the alarm clock summoning us to rise, to dashing for appointments and 'squeezing in' jobs, to rushing for deadlines, time – and the lack of it – makes itself felt and is uncomfortable.

Time becomes the byword for all that troubles us and causes us stress and annoyance. It takes us captive and makes us into its slaves. Hence we long 'to take time off', 'to have time for myself', and to be not 'working against the clock'. Indeed, the whole notion of a holiday has become for us the fixed time that we are 'let off' the normal strict demands of time. Conversely, if we have 'time on our hands', then we are bad or useless or both. So time – measured sequences outside of us – tells us what we should be doing, when we should do it, and becomes our accuser if we are not in its power.

Here we touch one of the enigmas of our culture: we can travel faster, produce quicker and communicate more speedily than ever, yet we seem to have ever less time. Part of the problem is that we have no perspective on time other than as a list of things to do and slots in a diary against which we allot tasks. Time has then become a commodity. Unfortunately, when this happens time becomes our master: for while we can make more of most other commodities, we cannot make more time. We may delude ourselves that we are making more time by re-allotting slots of time, but this only takes time from one task for another: there are still only a fixed number of slots.

Contrasting the view of time prevalent in the early Middle Ages with that of today brings two very different views of life into comparison, and gives us some insights into the way we live. We have mentioned this topic of time before now, especially in chapters 2 and 5, but here I wish to dwell upon it in more detail for through this topic we touch a basic strand of that earlier spirituality, and, in turn, of our own. We should begin by noting that there are many similarities – despite our romantic illusions about the past – between us and those people long ago which can make a comparison meaningful. First, we imagine that people long ago had more time or that in contrast to us they did not have to fill every moment of their day. However, a hundred years is a hundred years whatever moment you choose as its beginning, and those people were not struck by how much time they had, but its opposite. One of the most frequently noted remarks was that life was so

short, yet to learn how to do anything well took so long. We
have much more time: we live far longer, and we do not live
with the spectre of death anything like as close to us. Moreover,
their days were as filled with tasks that won't wait as are
ours: be that the *horarium* (routine daily schedule) of a monk
who had fixed times for prayer, or the routine of cooking and
feeding and child-caring, or the demands of milking and
calving and lambing. Hobbies are, after all, a modern phenomenon for the time that we have to spare. Second, we imagine
that there was less to do or that they did not have to work
long hours. Again, we imagine that the past was simpler. But
when we look backwards we tend to filter out the nasty bits,
so that the world then stands out in crisp and simple lines.
There was less variety of things to do, but most tasks took
longer than they do today. Whether we think of power tools
for the stone carver or carpenter, or ready-made butter and
electric ovens for the cook, or printed books and convenient
reference works for the scholar – everyone's tasks were more
time-demanding then than today: jobs were slower, the hours
were longer! Third, we think that they worked at a calmer
pace and were not 'busy'. In fact, while tasks could not be
accomplished with such speed, they still had to hasten to try
to fit everything in. We see this in the last lines of *De locis
sanctis* by Abbot Adomnán on Iona:

> I have described all these things for you – I admit some-
> what artlessly – despite the fact that each day brings an
> almost insupportable amount of ecclesiastical demands
> from every side and I have had to write the book amidst
> many laborious preoccupations . . . so do not forget to pray
> to Christ the judge of all times for me.

Executive stress is not new!

TIMES AND SEASONS

What is new is that while we think we make time, they thought
of themselves as living within it. One of the fundamental

texts for the whole of the Celtic Christian world was Genesis 1:14–18:

> And God said, 'Let there be lights in the firmament of the heavens to separate the day from the night; and let them be for signs and for seasons and for days and years, and let there be lights in the firmament . . . to give light upon the earth.' And it was so.
>
> And God made the two great lights, the greater light to rule the day, and the lesser light to rule the night; he made the stars also. And God set them . . . to give light upon the earth, to rule over the day and over the night, and to separate the light from the darkness. And God saw that it was good.

The structure of days, months and years, the movement of the heavens around them, and the seasons, was all there because of a direct command of God. Sun and moon, light and dark, day and night, hot and cold were there because God had built in such changes and sequences to the universe. To live as a creature on earth was to live in time, to exist within that rhythm. There was no need for a clock apart from that rhythm. The clocks they did use – such as sundials or the knowledge of when the sun or moon was visible in a particular place – were merely ways of checking the time in the great clock of creation. To be a human being, a creature of the sixth day, was to enter into a cosmos that was temporal, and indeed to live at the very heart of a great clock spinning around to tell one when to rise or lie down, when to sow and to reap (cf. Qoheleth/ Ecclesiastes 3:2), and when to work and when to rest (cf. Genesis 2:2).

This image from Genesis of the sun and moon being set there as the great lanterns and time-markers was not some alien religious imposition that had to be preached in the way we have to try to think ourselves into liturgical time or the notion that Sunday is special or Easter is a holy season. Wherever they looked there were confirmations of the basic truth

ROUND TOWERS AND SUNDIALS IN IRELAND

The monastic community in ordering time was redeeming it: the regularity of prayer and work restored human movement to the rhythm placed in the creation in its first moments.

of Genesis that 'seasons and days and years' were of God's fashioning.

At the level of the body they recognised that there were rhythms which reflected the time within the creation. Ageing and menstruation were the most obvious: one keeping time with the sun's annual circuit, the other with the moon. These were the same cycles that marked off movement in life, and were also the basic cycles that were used to discover the true times for celebrating the great act of the Lord's deliverance: Easter. There was, as Scripture told them, 'a time to be born and a time to die' (Qoheleth/Ecclesiastes 3:2). The whole of life was perceived as fitting into 'ages' which reflected in the individual the sequence of 'ages' in the universe. Pregnancy was a fixed amount of time (celebrated liturgically for both Christ and John the Baptist), then the time for first teeth, and then the times to the different stages of growth to adulthood – all seen as divinely appointed, numbered measures. Sickness and health too followed the seasons, as did the work to be done and its exhaustion. Yet at every moment the Lord could give or take away (cf. Job 1:21). The clock that was within the body ran in parallel to that outside – a thought we find so attractive – but it revealed in its sensitivity to sudden change its dependence on the will of God. When someone in midwinter on Iona or one of the other island monasteries read, 'For here we have no lasting city, but we seek the city which is to come' (Hebrews 13:14), they did not just hear a text recalling their eschatological destiny, but one which spoke immediately to their daily existence.

The clock of life was also visible in the basic activity of food production. The people of the Celtic lands lived within the cycles of nature in a way that even those involved in agriculture do not live today. The seasons produced the times for sowing and reaping, the times for shearing and milking, and one worked within those cycles or starved. Early medieval Celtic peoples lived far closer to famine through just a single localised crop failure than we can imagine. The problems such as we hear of in Africa today when a bad season can lead to a famine were part of their ongoing worries. It is from within that perspective we have to hear of the blessings of fields and crops and livestock. It is with such fears in mind we have to hear of people reciting the litanies as they walked around the fields and prayed for God's protection and a good harvest. The Irish annals record bad years for crops and animals, and record the taking of relics 'on circuit' to invoke the protection of the patron saint of that place. Adomnán records that because an area in what is now southern Scotland was under the protection of Columba, it was protected from plague. Even in good years, each foodstuff was limited to its season, and seen as the special gift of that season. We find it hard to remember an act of thanks for the 'gifts' on our tables and for those who do say a grace (literally translated, 'a thanks') it is a conscious religious act – it came far more easily when every meal was hard won, and could have been lost. By contrast our visit to a fast-food outlet for 'a burger, fries and shake' is an act almost wholly devoid of a specific time signature – it does not vary with season, or time of day, or weather, or what happened last year, or from one valley to the next, and equally it is harder to feel that 'your order' is just one more benefit from an omnipotent God.

At a less personal level than the body and its sustenance, there was a consciousness of the movement of the heavens which we simply do not need to notice. The regularity of the moon – which they heard praised nine times each week in the psalms (e.g. Psalm 8:3) – was a sign of God's steadfastness (Psalm 136:9); it would mark time until the end of the material universe (Psalm 72:7), but it would also determine how much light there would be for the monk's steps as he made his way from his cell to the oratory for the night offices. The amount of light was something they noted with care, and with it what constellations were visible and where on the horizon. This not only marked the year passing with its different tasks, but the times of the offices and the need for candles and lamps. This is an attitude to the year and its shifting seasons that does not affect us. Today liturgy still uses candles; in some places these are still blessed or there are special ceremonies for lighting them – and there is still the great ceremony for the Paschal Candle – but while these rituals can still touch us with their beauty, the notion that they touch upon the basic human realities is lost on us. For us to light a candle is a peripheral act; to someone who knows the amount of light that is due for that time of year, who knows that a lamp is a poor imitation of the great lights of heaven, and that this lamp is needed so that prayer or work can take place at these times of divinely ordered darkness, then lighting it is not just symbolic in some distant sense, but an act which, when performed liturgically, consciously enters into the purposeful movement of the universe.

The basic human sense of time is that of the alternation of day and night, light and dark, work and rest. This has been the case for people everywhere; we see it in the way our clocks and watches are made to mark time in relation to day or night (12-hour clocks) or the cycle of day and night (24-hour clocks). From the very beginnings of Christianity, part of our inheritance from Judaism, the day gave a basic shape to prayer. The *Didache* (mid to late first century) assumes that the Our Father (what would later be called 'the Lord's Prayer') will be said by Christians three times a day: morning, midday and evening. Later, more elaborate daily prayers grew up, and most elaborate of all was the daily order of prayer among monks where the celebration of the daily office became a central feature and purpose of their lives.

A saint like Augustine could marvel, throughout his life, at the beauty of the sun at dawn, and he praises the crispness of the African light in contrast to the less intense light of Italy. Meanwhile, in the East, Basil can be struck by the order of light and darkness as being a call to pray, and praises the hymn 'O light of evening' (*Phos hilaron*) as so old that no one knew when it was written. Both the dawn and the evening star spoke to these men of Christ and they used these images as key metaphors for the presence of the Saviour in human life. However, for Christians in Celtic lands all these images took on new qualities for both dawn and dusk are different the more one moves north: now there is the more gentle coming of day and it departs more slowly with twilight. This phenomenon is even more pronounced for those who live in the British

Isles surrounded by the sea. Likewise, the seasons took on a far more visible aspect. In the Mediterranean lands the difference in the amount of light at a solstice was only a matter of a couple of hours, but at Iona the difference between the amount of sun on 21 June and 21 December is almost twelve hours! The Lord had set the times and seasons in the heavens – and it touched every aspect of life and living. One can imagine a monk on Iona or Skellig Michael or Lindisfarne wondering how anyone could fail to see these movements of times and seasons as central to the life God established for his creatures.

When I was a child in the 1960s I remember visiting old relatives in rural Ireland. When the electric light was switched on, the man said, 'God give us the light of heaven!' I took electricity for granted, yet it had only arrived in that house in the previous decade and customs from the time of lamps and candles still survived. The moment impressed itself on my memory for everyone in the house, including my parents, could chime back 'Amen' in unison – but I had not heard this happen before. It is a liturgy of just two lines, but it linked that day, and that physical light, with a future 'day' and the notion of the incomprehensible light of God. When we speak of a sacramental understanding of the universe, it is that simple kitchen liturgy that we should keep in mind. For those people there would have been little need to explain with words 'the symbolism' of candles in the liturgy; every time they lit lamps, they knew that somehow they pointed toward heaven, and that to speak of heaven using lamps and candles made perfect sense, the action *now* in this reality was a petition for a *future* in another reality. It was many years before I recognised the richness of that simple act in a kitchen lit by one light bulb, but there were the last spontaneous traces of an attitude to life that makes those insular Christians of long ago so interesting to us.

paidir do ghaeilgeoirí

a thiarna, labhair tú leis na
ciníocha ina dteangacha dílse
féin domhnach cincíse. labhair
tú fós le muintir na héireann
ina dteanga féin trí phádraig,
bhríd, cholm cille agus naoimh
uile ár dtíre. soilsigh ár
n-aigne chun urraim a thabh-
airt don oidhreacht uasal a
tháinig chugainn tríd an
teanga sin, agus neartaigh ár
dtoil chun í a shlánú agus a
láidriú chun do ghlóire féin
agus onóir na héireann. trí
chríost ár dtiarna.

□□□□□□□□□□□□□□□□□□□□□□□

permissu ordinarii dublinensis

athchlo as an Timire

THE ONWARD MARCH

While our close-up sense of time is that of cycles, days, weeks, months, years, and the hands keep going round and round on the clock, we also know that time is running on in one direction. We are all getting older, the past is past and will not return, and we cannot go back and live our lives differently: time is like an hourglass that cannot be inverted again! To the physicist this is the movement running from Big Bang to Big Crunch, but for most of us it is the saga of passing youth and increasing grey hairs. Here again we have an experience which allows us to engage with those Celtic Christians of the first millennium.

Time belonged to the creation and marked a steady movement in just one direction from the beginning (as recounted in Genesis) until the End (which Christ had foretold in the Gospels). Time ran between the Alpha and the Omega (cf. Revelation 1:8 and the Easter Liturgy). Basil the Great, whose work on creation was known throughout the West in translation, had imagined the timespan of the creation as a giant water clock. It was full at the beginning and was steadily running out until the last moments when would come 'the judgement of this creation by fire' (cf. 2 Peter 3:5–7). This phrase as a description of the End became a commonplace as the liturgy used it in almost every blessing. But this one-direction line was not just a bland 'ticking' of one day following another, rather periods of time had different qualities depending on where they were located in the movement of history towards Christ reigning over all.

The world had progressed through the long ages of waiting for the Christ, now it was in the final times between his coming and his coming again to judge the living and the dead. This sequence of 'the law of nature', 'the written law', and then 'the gospel' was not just something in the history of Israel and then of the Church, it was a sequence of stages through which their own history as peoples had progressed. Thus they could arrange their past against an absolute time-line – as happened in every monastery for one of the tasks of the monastery was to keep annals which recorded significant events of each year of the Lord, but whose opening pages began with the first age recounted in Genesis. But those Celtic Christians also imagined and arranged their native past as a sequence of having just the insights that could be derived from nature, followed by a formal acknowledgement of a coming greater revelation (this can be seen in Muirchú for the Irish and Bede for the Anglo-Saxons, both drawing on Acts 17:22–31), followed by hearing the gospel, and the time of faith.

We noted already how people in early medieval societies perceived their lives pulsing to the same rhythm as the great clock that surrounded them, but they could also lay the span of their lives along the line of time that ran from the beginning to the end. For us to say that someone lived from AD 750 to AD 800 is simply to mark their life against a scheme which allows us to know 'before' and 'after'; for them it was between two determined points, each year was a God-given unit, situated at a particular stage within a whole pattern of divine activity which began with the 'let it be' of Genesis 1:3 and ended when the Lord would present the kingdom to his Father (cf. 1 Corinthians 15:24).

Against such a view of history, past, present and future, the life of the individual takes on a worth and significance that has been all too often forgotten in recent times. It obviously brings into sharp focus the eschatological notions of Patrick and other religious writers, but it also affected every Christian. First, it made the notion of Christ's advent and his interest in humanity and human activities far more real. His coming had changed their lives, for they, unlike their ancestors, lived in *his* time. His interest lay in their working within his time in the movement towards the Omega – it is not the interest of the watchful Lord keeping track of whether people were law-breaking that post-Reformation Christians would associate with the idea of the Lord being interested in their doings. Second, it invokes a different understanding of baptism to the ones with which modern Christians are familiar. The moment of baptism was that of moving from one 'time zone' (that which waits for Christ's coming) to another (namely, Christ's time). Baptism plunged the person into the time of the Saviour, just as surely as the Paschal Candle, with the year's date set between Alpha and Omega, was plunged into the water in the baptismal font on Easter night. Third, it meant that people could not just treat one block of time as equivalent to another, for each year was a particular point in a sequence. The individual's place in that sequence, the time from birth to death, was allotted by providence, and could not be seen as accidental. Today we find Jesus' statement about the sparrows in Matthew's Gospel hard to appreciate: 'Are not two sparrows sold for a penny? And not one of them will fall to the ground without your Father's will. But even the hairs of your head are all numbered. Fear not, therefore; you are of more value than many sparrows' (10:29–31). But for those earlier Christians it was little more than a statement of fact. Each day was numbered, and they were there by God's grace. Lastly, while we all have a sense of time passing by, of its ebbing away and disappearing never to return, our reactions today and those of earlier Christians are different. For Christians in the first millennium, it was a case that time was running out on them and on the whole creation; for us today the perception is almost completely the reverse: we are running out of time. In that subtle shift of perspective we have a key part of the difference between the past and now.

TIME AND TIME AGAIN

While we all age – experiencing time as a linear progression – we measure that progress by recurring birthdays: time as an annual cycle. But today – with the exception of the annual holiday, the birthdays of those close to us and anniversaries of significant moments of our personal journey – cyclical time is almost wholly threatening: the AGM, the annual audit, the monthly or yearly sales figures, the annual review of performance or contracts, the end of the tax year, the deadline for tax

returns ... Sometimes the annual sequence seems to over-
whelm us and we cry in sad jest: 'Stop the world, I want to
get off.' The last vestiges of a Christian sacral cycle –
Christmas and, for some, Easter – are little more than holi-
days. Work cycles and work time equal reality; other times are
just 'breaks' from that reality. Christians until recently still
took serious notice of Lent and Advent, but today when most
Christians hear of something like the Muslim period of fasting,
Ramadan, it is something from another world rather than an
analogue of something we ourselves know.

For Christians in the Celtic lands to live through the year
was to be submerged not in just one annual cycle of seasons
and liturgy, but in a whole series of such cycles which were all
interrelated and influenced one another. At the most basic
level here was the clock of the heavens setting out the seasons,
this affected the light around them, and so the length of different parts of the office. Then there was the agricultural year,
which brought with it the liturgy that was linked to the fields
such as the Greater and Lesser Litanies, the blessing of crops
and animals, and the recognition that each species brought
forth its fruit 'in due season' (Galatians 6:9).

Then there was the annual round of saints' days. This
brought into the life of each day Christians from every period
and place – strange names of people and far away places such
as we find in the calendar of feasts written in verse near
Dublin in the early ninth century, the *Félire Oengusso*. Here
is a sample for 27 July:

> The day of the bed-death of Simeon the monk,
> he was a great sun to the earth;
> with the suffering of a loveable host in Antioch high and
>   vast.

All they knew about this Simeon was his name, and that he
was a monk. They also knew that 27 July was the anniversary
of the martyrdom of a group of Christians at Antioch – which
Antioch they did not know. But Simeon and those martyrs
were brothers and sisters in the communion of saints and so

their memory was recorded and their intercession requested. There were also the local saints and patrons to whom one was not only related 'in Christ' but by family ties. All the early abbots of Iona, for example, belonged to the same tribe, as Columba himself, the Uí Néill. The day of death was seen as the birthday to the life of heaven. The dead whose destiny in heaven was held to be certain were asked for their aid, while prayers were offered for the eternal rest of those whose conversion to the fullness of Christ seemed less complete at the end of their earthly journey. All around the countryside lay the markers to these groups: wells preserving the names of the local saints, and stones marking graves with the inscription '[Make] a prayer for . . .'.

Then came the great cycle of the feasts of the Lord, each with its period of preparation and its period afterwards which extended the feast. The greatest of these days was Easter, and its date was determined by the very movement of the heavens: the Sunday after the full moon after the vernal equinox. When there were disputes about the mathematics of this calculation it was not simply a matter of liturgical regulations, but that the liturgy in one place be in harmony with that of Christians everywhere and with the very clock of the creation. Alas, their sense of the harmony that should exist between the liturgy of earth and heaven far outstripped the accuracy of their arithmetic. The problems of dating Easter, upon which wise heads such as Columbanus, Cummean and Bede spent so much time and effort, would not be settled until the 1580s when to solve the problem it would take not only better observations than had ever been made prior to then, but a completely new mathematics.

Within all these annual cycles came the lesser cycles of the week and the day, with each hour allotted to work or prayer. This daily round made time holy, and in the moments of prayer the activity of the little group became part of a much larger group whose liturgy did not cease for they were beyond the alterations that came with life in time. Time offered the possibility of chiming in with the court of heaven, and singing with one voice with the saints and ranked orders of angels. We should keep the image of the monastery sundial in mind to appreciate this. At the simplest level it was a clock to fix the time for the midday prayers: terce, sext and nones. But it actually announced these times by locating the time in direct accordance with the heavenly God-given clock whose purpose was that of setting the times of prayer. The heavens themselves told forth the glory of God and proclaimed his handiwork (cf. Psalm 19:1) – a fact the monks learned in the very psalms they were reciting on earth. This whole cycle of timed praise under heaven was but a reflection of the praise of an altogether higher world unlimited by time.

FEASTS AND FASTS

For most of us today there are really only four categories of time: bad times, work time, time off, and party time. For many even these four time-settings are more than they usually use: there is work time and time off, and a couple of extremes at either end which only cut in irregularly. This is a product of industrial and urban living over the last few centuries whereby in winter or summer we have the same pattern of day and the same deadlines to meet. The earlier cycle was based around variations over an entire year and so throughout the cycle there were events which would not return until that point next year. We have a cycle of variety where day follows day, or week follows week, while for earlier Christians the cycle was year following year. The penitence of Advent gave way to the feasting of Christmas. Then came the work of January followed by the beginning of Spring on 1 February. This was determined in Celtic lands by the amount of light: 1 February is roughly mid-way between solstice and equinox. This had been a feast, Imbolc, in pagan times, and now much of its imagery became part of the cult of Brigid whose feast fell on that day, while part of its imagery was transferred to the next day, Candlemas, with its great procession – looking forward to the year with its blessing of candles, yet looking back to Christmas forty days before. Soon after that came the boisterous time, 'the carnival', preceding Ashes and the serious time of Lent. But even Lent had its ups and downs: ups such as Laetare Sunday (surviving vestigially as Mothers' Day) and downs such as the Rogation Days.

And so the pattern went on, high days and low days, feasts and fasts, the ceremonies that came each day and the ceremonies that only came once each year. Penitence and fasting, rejoicing and feasting: the year reflected the whole of life and gave a form within which it was lived.

HARMONIES

The existence of time was seen as an invitation to settle oneself into harmony with the whole creation on its journey from the Beginning, when it came into being, to the End when Christ would be 'all and in all' (Colossians 3:11). The human life that was now out of harmony with that great journey was lost. Such a life was not aligned with the life of Christ and so was not heading towards the intended destination. At the everyday level, equally, there was a crucial need to fit one's life into the time of the universe. Without harmony between one's work and that of the seasons, one starved; without harmony between one's cycle of prayer and that of the heavenly court, one was simply muttering on one's own. The voyagers with Brendan become fit for entry into the land promised to the saints precisely by training themselves to be in perfect harmony with the times of the liturgy here, and so in tune with that of the heavenly Jerusalem. Time was temporary; it allowed people to set out on the journey to follow Christ until they reached 'to maturity, to the measure of the stature of the fullness of Christ' (Ephesians 4:13) and it would continue 'until the full number of the nation has come in' (Romans 11:25), and 'then comes the end' (1 Corinthians 15:24).

9. COMPARING TRAVELS

UNCOVERING ANCIENT ROUTES

Looking back at the spirituality of an individual who left a body of writings or of a group who had a self-conscious identity gives the historian a boundary around what he or she wants to examine, and also provides a basis for making a comparison with another spirituality so that the distinctive features of each come into view. That has not been possible in this book, for the Christians of the British Isles in the first Christian millennium had no such sense of spiritual identity. They wanted to be Christians, first and last, and would have rejected any notion that they were in terms of their Christianity in any way distinctive; that would be to put a separation between them and the rest of the Body of Christ, and so with its Head. We are so used to the idea of a fractured Christianity that we can no longer understand that horror of particularity. So if we notice variations between them and other Christians, it is something that we spot only with hindsight. However, what we see as distinctive in them is what distinguishes them *from us*, and only very rarely distinguishes them from other people living in the Latin West at the time. Thus many of the elements of the Christianity of the Celtic peoples looked at in this book may simply have come to notice because we are looking at the Celts; the same features may have been equally part of the spirituality of the Franks, Lombards and Visigoths but we have never chosen to look at the religious remains of these peoples.

Another difficulty that has beset this book is that when we

look at a group of hermits or monks we can put them into a distinctive category and note how they relate to other defined groups. But we have been looking at the remains of a people: some of these remains deal with monks, some with lay people, and some come without any specification. Moreover, they are scattered over several languages and over a lengthy period of time. We can only pick up a few themes and explore them under a handful of headings.. This may disappoint many readers, but a systematic presentation of aims, ideals and structures, such as many books present in the history of spirituality, is simply impossible. The materials are too scattered and too sparse. So this is not the account of the 'Celtic spiritual way', much less the 'spiritual journey of the Celts' – not enough evidence has survived for anything approaching such coverage. Several writers have attempted such books, or even claimed to have written them, but it is simply a delusion for that task supposes that we have plenty of relevant evidence, and that the Celts were sufficiently distinct as Christians for their 'way' to have stood out at the time as a conscious alternative.

Many have, of course, argued for such distinctiveness and have made much of the incident in Bede's *Historia ecclesiastica gentis anglorum* 3.25, now commonly called 'the Synod of Whitby' but which was then called Strenaeshalc. This has been seen as a clash of two conflicting ideologies, theologies, spiritualities, and even churches. In fact it was a meeting to iron out agreements on technical matters of discipline and involved no theological disagreements. Such meetings often took place, all over Christendom, in the period before the twelfth century, to get what we would call an agreed *modus operandi*. The only difficult matter was about the calculation of the date of Easter, but in this there were more divisions among 'Celtic Christians' within Ireland, and between Ireland and Iona (as Bede carefully pointed out), than between the 'Celtic Christians' and the 'Roman Christians' at Strenaeshalc in 664. Alas, this whole cult of the distinctiveness of the 'Celtic Church' in discipline and belief is a projection of the modern divisions and sectarian rivalries between Christian groups on to a time when all the Christians of an area could sit down to discuss differences in discipline lest, as Bede says, 'minds and hearts be troubled'.

If a distinctive 'Celtic way' in spirituality is illusory, what have we got from those people whose saints we admire and whose descendants many of us are? I suggest that what we can find is that they travelled roads – for there was not a single 'Celtic spiritual journey' but many intersecting journeys by people who were Celts – which are strange to us and only cut across our favourite paths here and there. However, just as we have much in common today, in that we share a language, many values within our society, and, by and large, a world-view, so did they. Each Celtic people had a common language and culture, they shared the same image of where they lived in the world, and through Latin had a language which allowed them to exchange ideas with Christians far and wide. Moreover, the way that Christianity was lived and preached in those centuries was very different from the way it is perceived and lived by us. Hence, while an Irish eighth-century monk had a different view of his life from one in the sixth century, from our perspective what both have in common in contrast to us stands out in sharper relief than what separates each from the other. Thus, all those different insights from people in Celtic lands on the western fringe of the 'known' world (whether they are unique to them or not) can be held up to us as a mirroring of one spirituality over against another. It is from this viewpoint, of holding the past as a mirror to the present, and vice versa, that I have written. So can we gather together some general points from this exercise of looking at Christians from that distant past?

DISCOVERIES

When we look back to those earlier times, perhaps the most interesting aspect of their spirituality is their sacramental understanding of the universe. To most modern Christians, if 'sacrament' means anything, it is in terms of a fixed number of discrete rituals that one does or has done to one. They hang in mid-air: they have a 'function' that is somehow 'independent' of the individual and so seem less authentic than our spontaneous prayer, yet at the same time they have an objective quality which makes them 'intermediaries' between human beings and Christ – and when that is mentioned, there is the fear that they will be perceived magically. The root of the problem is that we have kept bits (the two, or seven, or whatever number of sacraments) plucked from a larger tapestry which we have jettisoned as outdated. In the earlier perception of the universe there was a unified view of the whole creation as coming from God and returning to God. Coming forth it revealed his glory, and in returning offered him praise, and so any part of it, and every action within it, was *significant*, that is, it had a divine sign value and was part of a communication of God that was not simply words or special rituals, but the totality of our human experience. Within that embrace of divine communication there were the special moments: the moment of joining with Christ (Baptism) and sharing in his life (the Eucharist), the moments of marriage, religious profession, sickness, returning and preaching, where the signs took on an explicit shape ordered to the explicit communication of the Word becoming flesh. But they were not isolated from the background of God's communication to all humans at all times. We no longer look at the universe as a vast work of beauty doing its Creator's bidding, and telling of his goodness and power. As a consequence we are left with a book and some rituals: the Scriptures have become 'The Bible', a book written by people who did not share our world-view, so that increasingly we struggle to reach the realities of which its language offers signs. As for the rituals, for those who can still relate to them, they are often far distant from everyday concerns.

Recalling the spirituality of the early medieval period brings the creation back into focus, and in turn poses questions not only about how we react to the creation, but how we relate to the explicitly Christian signs such as sacraments and having scriptures. Many who are attracted to 'Celtic Christianity' are impressed by its 'holistic' approach and its concern for 'ecology'. In this they have, I believe, touched one of the valuable lessons we need to relearn. We could easily dismiss these interests by saying that neither word existed prior to the twentieth century, or that medieval people created just as much rubbish as any other group except they did not have our ability to use up materials at our rate. However, that objection misses the point. They did have a very different attitude to the creation, one which we can describe in terms of their own language and speculation as 'sacramentalist', but which today can be seen as intersecting with our notions of 'holistic living' and 'eco-friendly living'. Those Christians in the past were not ecology-conscious, but they did have a religious outlook which *de facto* shared many values with people today who are interested in ecology.

If the creation is a gift in its entirety and has the imprint of its origin in its order and beauty, and we have been placed in its midst with a purpose, then we have already a very different perspective to that of having matter simply around us, available for use in achieving our own goals. In the first case, the human being is the key element in the organism, and the interrelatedness of the whole is a piece of the handiwork of a loving God. In the other, the human being functions like a Greek god, a source of will and power who picks up matter to use and discard, and if there is a God then it is a distant 'god of gods' who has little to do with life here. In this scenario not only is matter without its divine imprint, but it is only valuable in so far as humans have used it.

From the religious perspective, if one lives in a sacramental universe, then whole debates within Christianity start to evap-orate. No longer does one have to identify 'the sources' of God's communication – for they are around us – and the emphasis moves to careful interpretation of that communication in all its varieties. The debate with other religions and traditions, or just someone else's experience, ceases to be one of 'marks out of ten' for getting some things right, and becomes instead a process of gathering the music of many tiny whispering instruments into the harmony of an orchestra. For over eight hundred years Christianity has struggled with the notion that revelation by God is something analogous to a complete set of mathematical theorems or the garage manual for a car. One effect of this has been to bundle Christianity up apart from the rest of life except in so far as it gives rules for what to do and what to avoid. When today we seek to perceive the holy in the everyday things, or recognise that spirituality must affect our whole way of living, then we are seeking the kind of experience that was a central part of Christianity for Eucherius of Lyons and those who followed him in the Celtic lands. In this view of life a walk down a country lane or a gathering with friends can help one make sense of Christ and his mysteries just as much as some obvious religious activity – and both the gathering of friends for a chat or the gathering for the Eucharist, or the walk down the lane to either the chat or the chapel, all belong to a pilgrimage of discovering the love that God has implanted in the creation, and which beckons us beyond it.

However, one of the greatest obstacles to recovering that older sacramental vision is the loss of a corporate understanding of human life. One of the central elements of the earlier spirituality was its sense that 'no man is an island'. For those earlier Christians, belonging to the Church was not an institutional affiliation, but a relationship to Christ and, so, to others. We can speak of believing 'in spite of the Church' or 'believing *and* belonging to the Church', but such options were not part of their world. This corporate sense meant that they perceived their labours as part of the work of a team, and they discovered how to learn about God within the cultural language of belonging to the Church. To believe was to be a disciple, and a disciple must have a master, and that master must stand in a tradition that reached back to the 'one Teacher, the Christ' (Matthew 23:10). Today we have a deep sense of individual identity, and so we speak of 'the Christians' meaning the collection of individuals who believe; but we have this at the price of collective anonymity. Who we are as a united group, and whether we can be such a united group, are questions which we face constantly, and which we are often afraid to answer. Earlier spirituality emphasised collective identity, sometimes even to the extent that it led to individual anonymity. One of the challenges that looking at the spirituality of the Celtic peoples poses to us is to recover a sense of belonging, of being the parts of the body of which Christ is the life-giving head. It reminds us of all the places in Christian tradition which emphasise that Christians must be one: one loaf at the Eucharist, one with Christ, one with each other, one with the poor, hungry and sick. The early Church emphasised in its preaching that to become a Christian was not the same as becoming a devotee of a philosophy or mystery cult, but rather it was to join a people, a team, a culture, and to throw one's lot in with that group so that the group's future would be that not only of the convert but of his or her offspring – from then on the children who would be born would belong to the 'people' called 'Christian'. The Celtic lands were among the last of 'the nations' to hear Christianity preached in this way and they retained that perspective for centuries. This is a foreign way of thinking for us, but it is one which has much to teach us as we seek to recognise the bonds that must unite us to peoples everywhere. Any real discovery of God must involve a discovery of obligations to our sisters and brothers. The earlier Christians in the Celtic lands expressed it by simply citing 1 John 4:20: 'If any one says, "I love God", and hates his brother, he is a liar; for he who does not love his brother whom he has seen, cannot love God whom he has not seen.'

The other major challenge that the Christianity of the early medieval Celtic peoples offers us – and this is something that is distinctive to them – is a view of sin and healing, and the idea that Christian living is a journey where we have to take up our pack each day and set out in discipleship. Christianity has always preached conversion/penitence/metanoia as its basic call, but equally it has always had difficulties with the idea of clearing the slate and starting again. This is a human need, and many who would not describe themselves as religious can acknowledge it as readily as those who do see themselves as religious, or who see some actions in their lives as sins. The insular practice of penitence was not perhaps the best possible, but it was a massive improvement on what went before it. It recognised that one did not become a disciple in one or two dramatic moves, but in a whole series, where 'downs' followed 'ups': the whole process should be seen as ongoing therapy rather than as a punitive repayment of debts.

Today, most mainstream Christian groups are comfortable with the notion of the Christian life as a pilgrimage, a journey that involves a slightly different route for each person. However, many still grapple with the problem of how to express that love of God which can enable the journey to begin afresh each day. In many Christian groups older means of highlighting sin and forgiveness have become dilapidated – one thinks of the decline to virtual extinction of the practice of auricular confession among Catholics – as these rituals no longer convey a sense of the love of God enabling a new start to be made in discipleship. This was the challenge that those early monastic pastors took up in Wales and Ireland in the late sixth century, and it is a task that will require equally creative courage from pastors today.

DISAPPOINTMENTS

Examining the documents that survive from the Church in Celtic lands in the first millennium can also bring a sense of disappointment. In one sense this is strange, for history is an investigation into what has already been rather than a hopeful search for something which might prove fruitful. The sense of disappointment comes from the hope that there was a golden age when all was as we believe it should be now. The longing for a golden past is an index of our heartfelt desires. Such a sense of disappointment used to be confined to those who imagined the early decades or centuries of the Church as 'the apostolic age', 'the age of the saints' or 'the age before the corruption', and who found they had to come to terms with the fact that disciples are always less than the master, and that it was to sinful disciples that the Lord came in the first place! Today a similar sense of disappointment affects some who go in search of 'the Celtic Church': they want to find people who had a simpler faith, who were inspired by beauty, who had a Christianity that was not encrusted with distractions and the debris of the past. However, the desire for a different Christianity here and now should inspire us to look to the past for explanations of how the current mess arose, and should encourage a bold creativity for the future rather than a melancholy search for a golden age. The harsh truth is that any age can appear golden with hindsight, for once we decide we like the feel of a period, we can subconsciously keep back the bits we like from what remains over from the blind sieve of time.

Discipleship is always a goal, not an achievement, while we are on our journey. When we look to the past it is to recall for us bits we have forgotten, point up bits that we were right to forget, and remind us that each generation has to work at building the Kingdom of God in its culture and time. In this last task the past may wag a finger at us, for previous generations may have been more successful in their day than we are in ours.

However, in the face of much contemporary romanticism about the Christian Celts, it is always a sobering thought to remember that the same minds which restructured the West's theology of sin as illness needing medicine is also the group who produced the first systematic corpus of canon law (the *Collectio canonum hibernensis*) and also produced the first set of scriptural proof-texts for the divine origin of the grades of the ecclesiastical hierarchy! So what is the distinctive contribution of the Christian Celts to the tradition: penitentials and systematic canon law? When one tries to think about this from within their perspective on sacraments and the Church, it is not nearly so negative as it may sound to our ears.

EDGES

For most of its history Christianity in Western Europe has been at the very centre of society: be that the village church which was the natural location of all the human rites of passage, or the place of the Church's hierarchy within the larger society with clergy forming one of the estates of the realm. In such situations the experience of being on the margins was a rare one for any Christian. Now that sense of being on the periphery is part of the spirituality of more and more Christians. One effect of this is that European Christians are looking to parts of their history where they might find a similar experience of being on the edges. While the earlier Christians in the Celtic lands did not have any experience similar to the current sidelining of traditional Christianity, they did live with the sense that they could easily be ignored by the people who lived close to the hub of affairs. They also had within their memories the time when their society had not yet heard of Christ, and had as part of their immediate agenda the need to bring Christ to peoples in parts of the British Isles and the European mainland who had not yet heard of him. Perhaps our own experience of being on the edge makes us respond to these earlier peripheral peoples in a way that we cannot with those who belonged to a church that was at the centre of things. Somehow we feel more comfortable with the church of Adomnán (d. 704) than that of Cardinal Richelieu (1585–1642): yet both were deeply involved in politics, both were fascinated by law, both were skilled theologians, and both wrote famous textbooks, one the *De locis sanctis* (*c.* 685), the other the *Instruction du chrétien* (1619). The religious world of both men is past, but it is that of Adomnán that attracts attention.

As we said earlier, many who search for 'the Celtic Church' are disappointed to find that it had bishops, teaching authorities, organised rituals, and a distinct fondness for canon law. We live in a world that sets a high value on individual freedom, yet at the same time we long for belonging. We fear involvements, yet we desire to be part of something that is greater than us individuals, something that can make a difference. It is curious that we are attracted to a period where identity was almost indistinguishable from belonging: one belonged to an extended earthly family such as the Uí Néill, and one belonged to an extended heavenly family, that of Christ. Since the Second World War one of the noticeable trends within Christianity has been the abandonment of the notion that to be Christian is to belong to the Church, yet at the same time interest has grown in things Celtic, which includes a spirituality with a more elevated notion of the Church, based on the Pauline body metaphors, than that of any grouping of Christians before or since. I appreciate that many have gone to look at Celtic material precisely out of a presumption that they would encounter a bishop-free zone – yet they have continued with their interest. Is this a sign of some deep underlying awareness of the need for community in faith, and indeed for a richer ecclesiology?

An important part of contemporary religious culture is that we have not 'arrived at the truth', we have not 'got the answers', but are trying to find our way amidst the pains and trials, discovering the signposts along the way. Life is a journey for which we do not possess a map, but only a compass, a conscience and some landmarks. In this process, faithfulness is the commitment to keep walking forward. To anyone who presents us with faith wrapped up (without doubts) in a box we cry out, 'God is ever more great!' At one level this is the very opposite of the experience of these early medieval people, who had a very definite attitude that in Christ they possessed the Way, the final Way, the perfect Way. However, in another respect they do speak to us, for they were deeply aware that life was a journey, and that they had to become skilled in reading the signs of his presence in the world around them, and to any who would think they had 'grasped' God, they too cried out, *Deus semper maior*.

To see ourselves, our society and the values that are evolving within that society is always difficult and it is even more difficult to see the religious trends moving within our society. However, by attempting to assess ourselves through our reactions to a past that is both foreign and familiar, we may discover parts of our religious selves that are otherwise invisible. Some of what we meet in the past or in our present will please us or flatter us, some of it will simply intrigue us in that we can be so different and still be Christians, and an occasional insight should pull us up sharply: no locality or period has mastered every aspect of discipleship. However, while it is useful to look backwards, and valuable to seek to understand other Christians who differ from us in outlook, we must neither take shelter from the challenges of today in the past, nor imagine that it can simply be reconstructed. For, as those Celtic Christians were so aware in their understanding of baptism, 'if any one is in Christ, he is a new creation; the old has passed away, behold, the new has come' (2 Corinthians 5:17).

A VANTAGE POINT

Studies of the Christianity of the Celtic people have a tendency to oscillate between extremes: in France in 1956 there was published a collection of essays devoted to early Christian Ireland entitled *The Miracle of Ireland* (ed. H. Daniel-Rops, English edn, Dublin 1959), and in 1967 came a rejoinder, in Italian, which asked whether it was a 'miracle' or a 'myth', and came down firmly on the side of myth. The pendulum has swung several times since then, and more recently between different extremes. There are those whose interest in the period derives not from a specialist interest in history but from a personal spiritual quest. On the one side are Christians who see in the Celts the answer to all our spiritual desires; in parallel to this, and despite the fact that all the written remains are Christian, some others have been able to find ancient 'nature cults', occult Gnostic wisdom, and the misty antiquity that does so much to give a whiff of intrigue to the cults of the New Age. Such exaggeration, lack of grounding in

the sources, and dishonest colonisation of the past by both
Christian and non-Christian enthusiasts has provoked a reaction that has wished almost to deny those early people any
spirituality or creativity in theology. If this were the case, the
Celtic peoples would become the first group who managed to
live the Christian life without it embedding itself in some way
within their culture, and the only group who were Christian
believers without generating a particular spirituality.

So can we draw together some general pointers? First, there
is a major problem of sources for the period. As a result we
must often situate those early Celtic peoples – as they so
wanted to do themselves – within the general religious framework of post-patristic western Christianity; and then, in
materials which we can source to the Celtic lands, take note
how those concerns are manifested. Sometimes we can detect
a more local flavour, at other times we can only detect the
religious attitudes that are common to the period.

Second, there were more localised spiritualities – every
social group has one – but we may not be able to discover them
from the scanty remains. However, this should be a reminder
to us that we too are generating a particular spirituality in
the local society in which we live; it too may never reach paper
or stone, and so will be forgotten. But we must reflect on
that local spirituality and calibrate it against other models of
discipleship.

Third, when we do look back at that period of over 500 years,
now more than a millennium ago, we must remember that we
are not dealing with one spirituality but many. The spirituality
of Ireland and the Irish parts of Scotland was different from
that of the Picts, and that of the Welsh, and Cornish, and
Bretons, and, as is more widely recognised, the Anglo-Saxons.
But equally they all interacted with one another: people and
books and ideas travelled between these places. Moreover, we
have material that comes from monasteries, each conscious of
its own traditions derived from its founder – what we would
call their 'distinctive spirituality' or 'foundation charism' – and
from other places besides. Some of the material was aimed

solely at those in holy orders, some at those involved in pastoral care, and some relates to ordinary Christian women and men who were working on the land, and some of it we just cannot tie down to any particular time or audience. So we should not talk about 'Celtic spirituality' but rather the spiritualities that are found in the Celtic lands.

Fourth, rather than seeking a 'miracle', a great mine from which we can extract answers to our problems, we should look to the past as a mirror which can help us now to explore our spiritual journey, for that past with all its differences is still part of the experience of Christians.

> *May we all reach the Kingdom of Heaven that is without end,*
> *may we deserve it,*
> *may we dwell there for ages unending. Amen.*
> (Conclusion of the Rule of the Céli Dé).

EPILOGUE

Sometime around AD 670, an Irish bishop named Tírechán set about collecting traditions about St Patrick. In his book, the *Collectanea* (section 26), he invents a scene of Patrick meeting the two daughters of the king of Tara by a well. One woman asks Patrick about the Christian God, and as his reply Tírechán puts the following statement of faith into Patrick's mouth. Its sources have never been located, yet it is a work that clearly bears the signs of use in the liturgy.

> Our God is the God of all humans.
> The God of heaven and earth.
> The God of the sea and the rivers.
> The God of the sun and moon.
> The God of all the heavenly bodies.
> The God of the lofty mountains.
> The God of the lowly valleys.
> God is above the heavens;
> and he is in the heavens;
> and he is beneath the heavens.
> Heaven and earth and sea,
> and everything that is in them,
> such he has as his abode.
> He inspires all things,
> he gives life to all things,
> he stands above all things,
> and he stands beneath all things.
> He enlightens the light of the sun,
> he strengthens the light of the night and the stars,

he makes wells in the arid land and dry islands in the
   sea,
and he places the stars in the service of the greater
   lights.
He has a Son who is co-eternal with himself,
and similar in all respects to himself;
and neither is the Son younger than the Father,
nor is the Father older than the Son;
and the Holy Spirit breathes in them.
And the Father and the Son and Holy Spirit are
   inseparable.

Patrick is then presented as offering her baptism with these
words: 'You are already daughters of an earthly king, I wish
to join you now to a heavenly king, if you choose to believe!'

FURTHER READING

So much has been written in recent years on religious topics with the adjective 'Celtic' that a survey of the material would take up many pages. Besides those that reflect the current religious interest, there are many works by medievalists and linguists dealing with the actual sources. What follows is only a small sample of many writings which can act as good introductions to the area.

Context

There are many fine introductions to particular Celtic lands in the early Middle Ages. A useful starting place is C. Thomas, *Christianity in Roman Britain to AD 500* (London 1981). On the culture of the Celts, and Celtic pre-Christian religion, there have been many studies in recent years. However, two works which combine accessibility with sound scholarship stand out. The first, presenting what we know of pre-Christian Celtic religion, is S. Piggott, *The Druids* (London 1968); the other, presenting an overview of Celtic society in Ireland in particular, is B. Raftery, *Pagan Celtic Ireland* (London 1994). Most works which present details of Celtic religion depend heavily on one important article: J. J. Tierney, 'The Celtic ethnography of Posidonius', *Proceedings of the Royal Irish Academy* 60c (1959–60), pp. 189–275. A related area of current interest is Celtic mythology, and the work of A. and B. Rees, *Celtic Heritage: Ancient Tradition in Ireland and Wales* (London 1961), is still a good starting point. For overviews of the history of the period and a general description of the societies, see M.

and L. de Paor, *Early Christian Ireland* (London 1958); D. Ó
Cróinín, *Early Medieval Ireland: 400–1200* (Dublin 1995); and
M. Richter, *Ireland and Her Neighbours in the Seventh Century*
(Dublin 1999). For a detailed window into everyday life, and
an introduction to the structure of early Irish society, F. Kelly,
Early Irish Farming (Dublin 1997) is indispensable.

Christianity and Society

On the more specific topic of how Christianity became the
religious core of these societies there are many works, each of
which adopt a slightly different perspective. For Ireland there
is the classic by K. Hughes, *The Church in Early Irish Society*
(London 1966). Approaching the topic from a literary angle we
have J. F. Nagy, *Conversing with Angels and Ancients* (Dublin
1997). For Scotland, there is a valuable collection of essays
edited by D. Broun and T. O. Clancy: *Spes Scotorum, Hope of
the Scots: Saint Columba, Iona and Scotland* (Edinburgh
1999). For Wales there is also a collection of essays, edited by
N. Edwards and A. Lane, *The Early Church in Wales and the
West* (Oxford 1992). And to fill out the picture by looking at
Christianity among the Anglo-Saxons there are H. Mayr-
Harting, *The Coming of Christianity to Anglo-Saxon England*
(London 1972) and P. Hunter Blair, *The World of Bede* (London
1970).

Sources

There is no substitute for reading what was actually written by
the people themselves. Unfortunately, in many cases, reliable
editions of the texts are hard to come by, and many anthologies
present the texts with little attention to context. For Irish
material – but including much of Welsh, Scottish and Breton
interest – there is the guide to the sources by J. F. Kenney,
The Sources for the Early History of Ireland: Ecclesiastical
(New York 1929). A useful anthology of texts relating to Iona
has been conveniently gathered by T. O. Clancy and G. Márkus,

Iona: The Earliest Poetry of a Celtic Monastery (Edinburgh 1995). Another anthology, providing much otherwise untranslated material, is J. Carey, *King of Mysteries: Early Irish Religious Writings* (Dublin 1998). However, one of the most wide-ranging anthologies is that of L. de Paor, *Saint Patrick's World* (Dublin 1993).

The Saints

One of the easiest ways to enter the religious world of the insular area is through looking at the saints. Here the writings of Patrick and Columbanus – where we read their own words – must have first place. For Patrick the most convenient place to find his works is my own *Saint Patrick: The Man and His Works* (London 1999). For Columbanus there is a bi-lingual edition by G. S. M. Walker, *Sancti Columbani Opera* (Dublin 1957) – it must be used with care, however, as it includes several texts which scholars no longer attribute to Columbanus.

There is also hagiography and modern studies of individuals. While the last century saw much ink spilled over the cult of Patrick and Brigid, Columba of Iona is currently the best served with books. There is an excellent translation of Adomnán's *Vita* by R. Sharpe, *Adomnán of Iona: Life of St Columba* (Harmondsworth 1995); and (in addition to the collection by Broun and Clancy, *Spes Scotorum*) there is a collection of studies edited by C. Bourke, *Studies in the Cult of Saint Columba* (Dublin 1997). For Adomnán himself, see T. O'Loughlin (ed.), *Adomnán, His Law, and Birr 697* (Dublin 2000). However, before setting out to read early medieval lives one needs an introduction to the literary genre of hagiography. The best guide is H. Delehaye, *The Legends of the Saints* (the most recent edition (Dublin 1998) points out some of the problems in Celtic hagiography). For a wide-ranging introduction to Breton, Cornish and Welsh hagiography, see K. Jankulak, *The Medieval Cult of St Petroc* (Woodbridge 2000).

Holy Places

Part of the fascination with the early Christianity of the Celtic peoples is the physical remains of their monasteries and other religious buildings. In terms of guides to these monuments which combine accurate information with convenience, Ireland is far better provided for than other places. Two good guide books which complement each other's coverage are P. Harbison, *Guide to the National Monuments in the Republic of Ireland* (Dublin 1970), and *Historic Monuments of Northern Ireland*, produced by the Department of the Environment for Northern Ireland (Belfast 1983). For a guide which also introduces the whole religious culture there is K. Hughes and A. Hamlyn, *The Modern Traveller to the Early Irish Church* (London 1977) – this is one of those books for anyone interested in Christianity in Ireland. Another useful book by P. Harbison is *Pilgrimage in Ireland: The Monuments and the People* (London 1991) which looks at both medieval and modern Christianity. And on the specific subject of High Crosses see H. Richardson and J. Scarry, *An Introduction to Irish High Crosses* (Cork 1990).

Theological Perspectives

There is no convenient general history of theology in English. In its absence, the works of J. Pelikan, *The Christian Tradition 1: The Emergence of the Catholic Tradition, 100–600* (Chicago 1971) and *The Christian Tradition 3: The Growth of Medieval Theology, 600–1300* (Chicago 1978) continue to do basic service. On the monastic background in particular, see C. Stewart, *Cassian the Monk* (Oxford 1998). Introducing the topic there is a useful collection of articles edited by J. P. Mackey, *An Introduction to Celtic Christianity* (Edinburgh 1989). For works on specific topics there are the following: on liturgy, see F. E. Warren, *The Liturgy and Ritual of the Celtic Church* (London 1881; 2nd edn with introduction and bibliography by J. Stevenson, Woodbridge 1987) – which despite its age has still no rival; there is lively interest in the penitentials, with books by P. J. Payer, *Sex and the Penitentials: The Development of a Sexual Code 550–1150* (Toronto 1984) and H. Connolly, *The Irish Penitentials and their Significance for the Sacrament of Penance Today* (Dublin 1995); for their views of the world and Scripture see my *Teachers and Code-Breakers: The Latin Genesis Tradition, 430–800* (Turnhout 1999); for their perspective on evil, see J. Borsje, *From Chaos to Enemy: Encounters with Monsters in Early Irish Texts* (Turnhout 1996); and for an introduction to Eriugena, see by J. J. O'Meara, *Eriugena* (Oxford 1988). For an attempt to bring the discipline of historical theology to bear on religious texts from early Ireland, see my own *Celtic Theology: Humanity, World, and God in Early Irish Writings* (London 2000). Recent years have seen great interest in what the Christianity of the Celtic lands can offer modern believers, and the best guide to this is I. Bradley, *Celtic Christianity: Making Myths and Chasing Dreams* (Edinburgh 1999).

WORKS MENTIONED IN THIS BOOK

This book draws on a very wide range of sources, but what follows is simply a listing, in alphabetical order, of those texts to which I have explicitly referred here, so that passages I have quoted may be pursued *in situ*. I shall first list the insular sources and then the continental patristic sources from whom the insular writers drew inspiration. Where a work exists in an English translation, this alone is cited – although my translation may differ somewhat from that of the translation listed here.

INSULAR AUTHORS

Many authors, *Penitentials* (L. Bieler (ed.), *The Irish Penitentials*, Dublin 1975; Latin text with facing English translation).

Adomnán, *De locis sanctis* (D. Meehan with L. Bieler (eds.), Dublin 1958; Latin text with facing English translation).

Adomnán, *Vita Columbae* (A. O. Anderson and M. O. Anderson (eds. and trs), *Adomnan's Life of Columba*, Edinburgh 1961, 2nd edn Oxford 1991; and R. Sharpe (tr.), *Adomnán of Iona: Life of St Columba*, Harmondsworth 1995).

Anon, *Liber de ordine creaturarum* (M. C. Diaz y Diaz (ed.), *Liber de ordine creaturarum: Un anónimo irlandés del siglo VII*, Santiago de Compostella 1972; Latin text with facing Spanish translation).

Anon, *Nauigatio Sancti Brendani* (J. J. O'Meara (tr.), *The Voyage of St Brendan: Journey to the Promised Land*, Dublin 1976).

Anon, *Rule of the Céli Dé* (E. Gwynn (ed.), *The Rule of Tallaght*, Dublin/London 1927, pp. 64–87; Irish text with facing English translation).

Anon, *Stowe Missal* (G. F. Warner (ed.), London 1906 and 1915 (one vol. edn, 1989); Latin text without translation).

Anon, The Sermons *In nomine Dei summi* (R. E. McNally, ' "In nomine Dei summi": Seven Hiberno-Latin Sermons', *Traditio* 35 (1979), pp. 121–43; there is a complete translation in this book, and see T. O'Loughlin, 'The Celtic homily: creeds and eschatology', *Milltown Studies* 41 (1998), pp. 99–115).

Bede, *Historia ecclesiastica gentis anglorum* (B. Colgrave and R. A. B. Mynors (eds.), Oxford 1969; Latin text with facing English translation).

Eriugena, *Periphyseon* (I. P. Sheldon-Williams and J. J. O'Meara (trs), *Periphyseon: The Division of Nature*, Montreal/Washington 1987).

Eriugena, *Homily on the Prologue to the Gospel of John* (English translation in J. J. O'Meara, *Eriugena*, Oxford 1988, pp. 158–76).

Muirchú moccu Macthéni, *Vita Patricii* (L. Bieler (ed.), *The Patrician Documents in the Book of Armagh* (Dublin 1979), pp. 62–125; Latin text with facing English translation; and see the translation by T. O'Loughlin in O. Davies with T. O'Loughlin (eds.), *Celtic Spirituality* (Mahwah NJ 1999) which provides a scriptural apparatus).

Oengus mac Oengobann, *Félire Oengusso (The Martyrology of Oengus the Culdee*, W. Stokes (ed.), London 1905 (Dublin 1984); Irish text with facing English translation).

Patrick, *Confessio* (N. J. D. White (ed.), 'Libri Sancti Patricii; The Latin Writings of St Patrick', *Proceedings of the Royal Irish Academy* 25c (1905), pp. 201–326 for the Latin text; and see T. O'Loughlin, *Saint Patrick: The Man and His Works*, London 1999, for an annotated English translation).

Patrick, *Epistola ad milites Corotici* (as for the *Confessio*).

Tírechán, *Collectanea* (L. Bieler (ed.), *The Patrician Documents in the Book of Armagh* (Dublin 1979), pp. 122–67; Latin text with facing English translation).

NON-INSULAR AUTHORS

Athanasius, *Vita Antonii* (M. E. Keenan (tr.) in R. J. Deferrari (ed.), *Early Christian Biographies*, Washington 1952, pp. 127–216).

Augustine, *Confessiones* (F. Sheed (tr.), *The Confessions of St Augustine*, London 1945).

Augustine, *De ciuitate Dei* (R. W. Dyson (tr.), *Augustine: The City of God against the Pagans*, Cambridge 1998).

Augustine, *De doctrina christiana* (J. J. Gavigan (tr.), *Christian Instruction*, Washington 1947).

Cassian, *Conlationes* (B. Ramsey (tr.), *John Cassian: The Conferences*, New York 1997).

Eucherius Lugdunensis (of Lyons), *De contemptu mundi* (S. Pricoco (ed.), *Il refuto del mundo*, Fiesole 1990; I am not aware of an English translation).

Eucherius, *De laude eremi* (C. Wotke (ed.), *Corpus Scriptorum Ecclesiasticorum Latinorum*, Vienna 1894, vol. 31, pp. 178–93; I am not aware of an English translation).

Eucherius, *Formulae spiritalis intellegentiae* (C. Wotke (ed.), *Corpus Scriptorum Ecclesiasticorum Latinorum*, Vienna 1894, vol. 31, pp. 1–62; I am not aware of an English translation).

Jerome, *Vita Pauli* (i.e. Paul of Thebes, the First Hermit) (M. L. Ewald (tr.) in R. J. Deferrari (ed.), *Early Christian Biographies*, Washington 1952, pp. 219–38).

Jerome, *Vita Hilarionis* (Hilarion), (Ewald (tr.) in Deferrari (ed.), pp. 241–80).

Jerome, *Vita Malchi* (Malchus) (Ewald (tr.) in Deferrari (ed.), pp. 283–97).

John Cassian, see 'Cassian'.

John Scottus Eriugena, see 'Eriugena'.

Orosius, *Historiae aduersum paganos* (R. J. Deferrari (tr.), *Paulus Orosius: The Seven Books of History Against the Pagans*, Washington 1964).

Palladius, *Historia Lausiaca* (R. T. Meyer (tr.), *Palladius: The Lausiac History*, Westminster MD/London 1965).

Rufinus, *Historia monachorum in Aegypto* (This anonymous work was translated into Latin by Rufinus; the Latin text is most conveniently consulted in J. P. Migne, *Patrologia Latina* 21, pp. 387–462; I have not been able to find an English translation.)